PROMOTING CULTURAL DIVERSITY

PROMOTING CULTURAL DIVERSITY

STRATEGIES FOR HEALTH CARE PROFESSIONALS

Kathryn Hopkins Kavanagh
&
Patricia H. Kennedy

SAGE Publications
International Educational and Professional Publisher
Newbury Park   London   New Delhi

For information address:

SAGE Publications, Inc.
2455 Teller Road
Newbury Park, California 91320

SAGE Publications Ltd.
6 Bonhill Street
London EC2A 4PU
United Kingdom

SAGE Publications India Pvt. Ltd.
M-32 Market
Greater Kailash I
New Delhi 110 048 India

Printed in the United States of America

Library of Congress Cataloging-in-Publication Data

Kavanagh, Kathryn Hopkins.
  Promoting cultural diversity : strategies for health care
professionals / Kathryn Hopkins Kavanagh, Patricia H. Kennedy.
        p.   cm.
  Includes bibliographical references and index.
  ISBN 0-8039-4656-2. —ISBN 0-8039-4657-0 (pbk.)
  1. Transcultural medical care.   2. Medical personnel and patient.
I. Kennedy, Patricia H.   II. Title.
RA418.5.T73K38   1992
610.69'6—dc20   92-2235

        93   94   95   10   9   8   7   6   5

Sage Production Editor: Diane S. Foster

Contents

Foreword

Ever since Gregor Mendel first noticed genetic differences, we have known that the power, the efficiency, and the beauty of all living things is a function of their differences. Nature is a symphony of diversity, and therein lies its magnificence. It is interesting that we have noticed this and taken advantage of it in every living system with the exception of our own. Human beings have interpreted differences as symbols to fear.

It is not enough to know that diversity is the underpinning of the universe; one also must know the details of how it works itself out in mankind through individuals and society. The job of science is to look at these interconnections, not just to accumulate facts, but also to place facts within rational concepts and theories so that they have meaning and can be passed on in an orderly systematic way to increase the effectiveness of others who do not yet know or appreciate them. That is the function of this book.

This book is for anyone who has ever aspired to fully experience the variety that life has to offer. Have you ever marveled at the diversity in age, ethnicity, gender, physical size, and socioeconomic status of those clustered at a city street corner? Have you ever experienced discomfort with someone who is handicapped, homeless, of a different country, race, or religion? Perhaps you don't see the differences, or choose to pretend they don't exist, or just treat everyone alike regardless of their diversity. Appreciation of differences is not automatic. Most of us do not wish to be bigots or show prejudice, but we simply lack confidence and expertise in dealing with diversity through affirmation.

This book is for you if you have ever questioned your sensitivity, understanding, or handling of human differences. If you have never had such an experience, this book is especially for you. This is a book that will help each of us assess our own shortcomings and face the myths and stereotypes that cripple our ability to interact effectively with those who differ from ourselves.

This book was written particularly for health care professionals to help them recognize human differences, confront their own biases, identify their own deficits, and foster the development of awareness, sensitivity, knowledge, and skills required to provide affirmation of the diversity they encounter in their practice. It evolved from nursing faculty searching for ways to help each other understand and work through the human barriers to provide an educational environment where diversity could flourish. We wanted not only to open our doors to students, faculty, and staff of diverse backgrounds, but also to open our hearts and minds to the learning required to change prevalent attitudes and create an openness to the richness of diversity. This book was an outgrowth of the efforts of the authors and others to provide the background, challenges, and tools to initiate that process.

The authors themselves have diversity in personal backgrounds and life experiences. Their commitment to enrich understanding combined with the courage to confront the controversial made this book a reality. They value the influence of the educator and health care provider in producing societal change. They advocate a shift in the health care community from a "unicultural" approach to one that is sensitive to the population and provides for "culture specific" needs. They maintain that educators and health care professionals individually and collectively can interpret and reformulate models of belief, societal knowledge, and ideologies held by those in the health care system and society at large.

This book is not just a theoretical presentation to enhance understanding, but it also provides easy-to-use, practical approaches for the practitioner, the teacher and the student as a reference or as a text. Commonly held myths that will challenge the most magnanimous thinker are identified and addressed in detail. Case studies and scenarios provide excellent material for consideration, discussion, and analysis in the classroom or professional conference. The teaching and learning strategies will not only help the reader deal with diversity, but also with the controversial issues that, when ignored, only serve to perpetuate the discrimination and social inequities common to our society.

This book is unique in that it addresses inequity, prejudice, and discrimination by concentrating on the meaning of the experience and its developmental and cumulative effect at both individual and societal levels. Accompanying this opportunity for comprehensive understanding and self assessment, the reader is provided with strategies for appreciating and affirming human diversity. It is not an emotional book, but one cannot help but feel its profound impact and its potential for enriching one's own life.

Frieda M. Holt
Professor, School of Nursing
University of Maryland

Acknowledgments

Lawrence C. Johnson, Director of the Human Relations Program, University of Maryland, Baltimore County campus, is acknowledged for his insight, guiding questions, and other assistance with early versions of this manuscript.

The faculty and students of University of Maryland's School of Nursing are recognized with gratitude for providing the impetus for creating this manuscript and for their evaluation of earlier versions of the strategies for intervention presented in this book.

We also acknowledge the many students who presented us with challenging clinical scenarios that reflect the diversity of our nation and the world. Special recognition goes to Sharon Strobel, who, as a student, extended the effort required to cross cultural barriers, to understand social process in complex and subtle forms, and to provide the culture-specific care that "Nate" needed.

Introduction

Concern by health care providers about the challenge of providing appropriate care to increasingly diverse consumer populations has prompted greater exploration of ways to tailor care to clients' needs. There is a parallel effort to eliminate practices and policies that require consumers of health care to adapt and conform to a limited set of norms and values in order to utilize resources. All of this points to a need to understand diversity and to examine the repercussions of that variety in social process.

Diversity exists anywhere there is not homogeneity or sameness, although "differentness" in the United States tends to refer to divergence or deviation from a single standard, specifically that underlying Anglo- or European-American expectations and ideals. Diversity is often viewed as an assortment of contrasts and variations more closely akin to miscellany than to medley. In harsher terms diversity is frequently viewed as more of a liability than an asset. Regardless of one's opinion of diversity, however, it is generally acknowledged that, with differences rooted in age, culture, health status and condition, ethnicity, experience, gender, and sexual orientation, the variability and combinations are nearly limitless.

Concern about diversity is not new, although there is a fresh awareness that simply labeling differences is not adequate. Historically, responsibility for the atypical client (if accepted at all) tended to be apportioned by association to those providers who shared some similarity. For example African American health care providers were and still are frequently assumed to share commonalities with and accountability for all blacks, as if the same variability in values and beliefs that exists among European Americans does not exist among African Americans. Such expectations are in part the result of a limited repertoire of recognized options and limited enthusiasm for developing alternatives. Reflecting society at large, the health sciences, despite development of an awesome technology and overwhelming bank of knowledge, have invested relatively little in examining how we might better get along with each other. Few books and journals in the average medical library pertain to facilitating relationships and providing health care in ways that acknowledge diversity.

This book developed from watching students grapple with diversity. Some came convinced that diversity was, by definition, rich and rewarding (whether or not they knew how to reap rich and rewarding experiential outcomes). Others came resenting the complications imposed by clinical or collegial differences, which they almost inevitably viewed as liabilities. Relatively few knew techniques for systematically cultivating their sensitivity and bolstering their knowledge about human similarities and differences. Even fewer could identify pertinent and substantive behavioral skills.

We, the authors, noted that virtually every student whom we encountered during classes and discussions readily recalled (although sometimes had more difficulty articulating) incidents of social unease that they attributed to diversity. We also realized that few students felt confident that they had adequate knowledge and skills for effective intervention in those complex interactive situations or how to acquire those, although such situations occurred frequently. The students were, in other words, more aware and sensitive than knowledgeable and skillful. Their lack of confidence was displayed in their communication patterns, which tended to change when topics that they considered "sensitive" arose. Overtly ill-at-ease, they lowered voices, hunched shoulders, shuffled feet, diverted eyes, dropped books, got quiet, sought agreement with their ideas and feelings, and sent furtive glances (often to locate members of minority groups

—as if any discussion related to minority status was automatically offensive). Words they ordinarily handled with ease were stumbled over. They often became circumspect and expressed fear of "hurting feelings." Designations referring to race, ethnicity, poverty, or sexual orientation were likely to be avoided or reported in subdued tones.

It seemed that this avoidance pattern extended to nearly all unfamiliar situations involving diversity, and that recurring circumstances were handled by ignoring or minimizing differences. It was apparent that they did not feel it was acceptable to acknowledge and respond to differences. Avoidance behaviors were most pronounced in the description of uncomfortable compromises in which they had been involved or that they had observed. Students recognized that interactions sometimes overtly or covertly risked respect for personal integrity. Because they often did not know how to intervene gracefully in situations that involved diversity, some had chosen to avoid them. They used terms such as "being on thin ice" and "walking on eggshells" to symbolize their discomfort and unpreparedness. For them, diversity was a liability and differences were best not acknowledged.

When an individual student had been personally victimized in a situation in which he or she was invested (at work or school, for instance), the perceived risk in articulating and exploring the problem was even greater. African-American nurses described, for example, incidents in which other health care professionals had "looked right through" them to seek information from an untrained, albeit white, member of the housekeeping staff. Young providers had been "written off" for their age and "immaturity"; older individuals had learned that more years may not be interpreted as better. Some European-Americans were convinced that they were unfairly disadvantaged by Affirmative Action programs; some African-American health care workers felt rejected by European-Americans, some women by men, and the list went on and on. Many were sensitive, but few were prepared for situations that involved diversity. Most had learned to tolerate diversity, but not how to live with it in a manner that let them appreciate and value it. They did not know how to effectively manage themselves in a diverse environment.

Further impetus for development of *Promoting Cultural Diversity: Strategies for Health Care Professionals* came with the observation that, however blatant the situation may seem to outside viewers, the complexity and subtlety of social process often masks or alters its meaning for students and others who are actually involved. Unrecognized biases frequently truncate analytical processes prior to consideration of all aspects of a situation. For example, it is not uncommon for students to assume that societal or community homogeneity implies strength and cohesion, and that diversity equates with fragmentation and weakness. Entrapment by such uncritical assumptions precludes closer, objective analysis as well as openness to the richness of diversity.

Expounding on the rewards of diversity is not enough to increase awareness, knowledge, and skills. Basically, people must be equipped to deal with diversity. It took us several years to delineate the most useful techniques and content for promoting that ideal among members of health care disciplines. To build the sensitivity, knowledge, and skills that foster culturally sensitive action, frameworks were borrowed from cross-cultural counseling, in particular Paul Pedersen's work, and from transcultural nursing and Madeleine Leininger's contributions.

It is not the intent of this book to prepare readers to confront the innumerable differences they are likely to experience in interactions; that would be an impossible goal to meet. Instead, we present a framework for understanding social processes underlying the significance that is attached to differences (Brislin, Cushner, Cherrie, & Yong, 1986), and a set of strategies for communication and intervention to bridge the gaps formed by those differences. The theoretical stance employed is basically humanistic, with emphasis on the choices that individuals make (Gergen & Gergen, 1982), and social interaction at all levels. Social stratification is a reality in American society, and the distribution of power is the critical factor in determining social rank. This theoretical combination helps to explain the meaning of experience, and its developmental and cumulative effect at both individual and societal levels (Kim, 1988).

Methodologically, the approach involves introduction of sets of concepts, variables, and behaviors to which meaning must be assigned. Such meanings or inferences are essential for analysis and development of appropriate plans of intervention. The assignment of meaning uses present knowledge, attitudes, values, morality, and past experiences. Effective intervention requires a balance of sensitivity, awareness, knowledge, and skills (Pedersen, 1988). Transcultural nursing theory and intercultural communication theory provide the frameworks for intervention. This is based on the conviction that culture and communication shape reflections of everyday life and the construction of bridges to deep-seated beliefs (van Dijk, 1987; Damon, 1989).

This book presents concepts and strategies that are directly related to understanding, analyzing, promoting, managing, and affirming diversity. The promotion of diversity moves beyond tolerance, patronization, generosity, and "good deeds," and even beyond common decency, to confronting differences and developing the flexibility that allows appreciation and respect for both differences and similarities. Managing diversity means developing awareness, sensitivity, knowledge, and skills that encourage authentic, effective interaction, that is, interaction that is enhanced, rather than hindered, by differences. The terms "promotion," "affirmation," and "management" are used knowingly. The rationale for their use is based on the rationale that we are a diverse people and becoming increasingly so in this country. More than half the U.S. work force now consists of minorities, immigrants, and women (Thomas, 1990). The "browning of America" refers to projections that by the middle of the twenty-first century the average U.S. resident, as defined by Census statistics, will trace his or her ancestry to Africa, Asia, the Pacific Islands, or the Hispanic or Arab worlds, rather than to European roots (Henry, 1990). Diversity is what makes the United States unique. Diversity is here to stay, and America is learning to build on it, to appreciate its potential, and to validate and affirm it. The trend is away from social distancing (Dyer, Vedlitz, & Worchel, 1989), Affirmative Action, and a competition model toward promotion of diversity, that is, toward using diversity to develop everyone's potential and to every-one's advantage (Thomas, 1990).

Affirming and managing refers to encouraging and developing potentially productive and rewarding relationships that historically were curtailed due to social barriers and customs. "Managing" diversity is not manipulative or exploitative. It is facilitating development of full potential, whether that is measured in productivity, commitment, cooperation, quality, personal satisfaction, or profit. To the health care disciplines it means enabling health promoting behaviors in ways that might otherwise be lost in miscommunication between a provider's "imposition" and a consumer's "noncompliance." It means providing acceptable and culturally congruent care.

Diversity is not specifically about inequity, nor is this book. Ours is a positive, affirmative stance toward diversity. "Inequity" and "diversity" are distinct and independent concepts. Many circumstances involving diversity are fully equitable, and inequity occurs in numerous situations not characterized by obvious "diversity." Nonetheless, inequity, prejudice, and discrimination exist in both the immediate social context and the broader structure of society. Because social characteristics that typify diversity are associated with patterns of access to resources, including health care, discussion of inequity relates directly to that of diversity.

Discrimination, the behavioral expression of prejudice (Ritzer, Kammeyer, & Yetman, 1982), occurs when differences are used to the disadvantage of a group or person and to the advantage of the perpetrator. Discrimination against members of specific categories results in inequitable experiences and opportunities. The crucial distinction between the discriminator and the victim of discrimination is the relative power each has. Power, therefore, is a concept that will be explored in considerable detail in this book.

Referents to "students" and "clients" are used throughout *Promoting Cultural Diversity: Strategies for Health Care Professionals*. Students are learners, and learners may be anyone, with or without official designation of that status and role. It is also important to note that there is wide variation in how students learn as well as in how instruction is given (Sedlacek, 1983; Anderson, 1986, 1990; Hofstede, 1986) and in health care provision and utilization. "Client" is used here to differentiate health care consumers from providers. In actuality, providers are also consumers, and the material presented is not limited in applicability to the health care system. It is important to note, however, that for some cultural groups "client" is necessarily plural because problems are conceptualized as affecting the group, not individuals. It is, furthermore, not uncommon to provide care for couples, families, small groups, or even larger populations. "Client," used in its singular for the sake of simplicity, is equally appropriately pluralized.

It is expected that the legitimacy of the issues presented will be questioned by some. It is unlikely that its content will be viewed as automatically relevant to all segments of the population to whom health care is provided. Many of the topics discussed are considered controversial in a society that is as socially stratified as ours. It is anticipated that the material presented will be met with a myriad of responses. Some individuals may experience perceptions of dissonance that produce fear of exposure of inner feelings, values, or attitudes, and subsequently display resistance to the learning process. However, acknowledgment of attitudes facilitates understanding of social processes. The part that fear plays in the perpetuation of stereotypes is acknowledged, and suggestions are included for assisting with acknowledgment of those fears. Situations that involve diversity result frequently in discomfort with the very "differentness" that circumscribes diversity. Such unease encourages avoidance of or defensiveness in cross-cultural situations (Brislin et al., 1986; Pedersen, 1988). In that regard, we are all perpetual learners; none of us is free of bias or totally comfortable exploring unknown territories. We all can continue to grow, however, and we can learn the flexibility needed to value exploration as an opportunity. Positive intervention involving diversity requires practice.

Promoting Cultural Diversity: Strategies for Health Care Professionals was designed with nursing faculty and students in mind. The authors are interdisciplinary in perspective, however, being (between them) a medical anthropologist, an instructional systems specialist, an intercultural counselor, mental health clinical nurse specialists with experience with inner city and "minority" populations, a member of an ethnic "minority" group, and a member of an ethnic "majority" group, and longtime educators—with a combined total of about 50 years of clinical experience. We have made an effort to make the content appropriate to persons who interact in situations involving diversity in health care settings. Whether related to gender or sex roles, age, physical size or condition, socioeconomic status, race, ethnicity, national origin—or any combination of those or the many other mechanisms of social stratification—the issues and impact are similar.

Format of the Book

Part I of *Promoting Cultural Diversity: Strategies for Health Care Professionals* sets the stage for discussion and application of the issues that surround cultural, gender, ideological, and experiential diversity and its subsequent analysis. It includes a discussion of relevant theoretical material and its application in health care settings.

Part II focuses on communication skills and intervention strategies useful to effective management of care in situations characterized by diversity. A repertoire of experiential strategies and aids for teaching and learning about diversity is presented. Relevance of those exercises is not limited to faculty and students but, rather, extends to practitioners, because western health care professions depend heavily on health education as a mode of intervention.

Following the material presented in Parts I and II are sets of questions and myths for discussion. The myths are collections of commonly held beliefs that represent fallacious or negatively stigmatizing convictions. Myths contribute to the perpetuation of stereotypes and to inequitable social processes, creating barriers to the promotion of diversity. Because they are familiar, they may serve as initiation points for discussion, especially for readers who are uncomfortable with the dynamics of diversity.

Part III consists of a set of scenarios, collages, and an extensive case study that illustrates analysis of a complex, real-life situation. The scenarios are provided to prompt further application of the analytic process.

Summary

The Introduction to *Promoting Cultural Diversity: Strategies for Health Care Professionals* emphasized the health care professional's role as catalyst in preventing and decreasing social distancing that interferes with the provision of care, and as a potential enabler of communication and intervention that allows affirmation of diversity. The interdisciplinary orientation of the book makes its content appropriate for anyone who encounters situations involving diversity in health care settings. The overall plan of this book is to increase familiarity with cultural patterns and social processes, while decreasing fear of the unfamiliar and different by providing tools that empower effective communication and intervention.

Part I Conceptual Background

Reflecting a cultural system in which individualization and independence are highly valued, American health care has traditionally acknowledged and emphasized individuals as the locus of problems and of intervention. The influence of patterned cultural and subcultural characteristics, the symbolism and meaning attached to those characteristics, and the impact of those and other population-level factors have not been consistently incorporated into providers' knowledge bases.

Social Interaction and Communication

Society may seem chaotic at times, but it functions through ongoing, patterned interactions (Ritzer et al., 1982). It is in large part through communication and interaction with those around us that we become who we are, learn the patterns and approaches we use to interpret and deal with the world around us, and arrive at conclusions about the relative worth of others and of ourselves (Sullivan, 1937, 1953; Strauss, 1956; Blumer, 1969; Kuhn, 1964; Rosenberg, 1965, 1981; Schroeder, 1981; Gecas, 1982; Mecca, Smelser, & Vasconcellos, 1989).

Social interactions, like other behaviors, are driven by decisions (Goffman, 1956, 1967, 1969; Becker, 1963; Berreman 1962, 1973; Pedersen, Draguns, Lonner, & Trimble, 1981; Pedersen, 1988). Options and alternatives, no matter how they are shaped by specific cultures and perceived by specific individuals within those cultures, are weighed. Decisions are then made based on what is known, thought, or felt about the choices.

The communication of outcomes of the decision-making process is through language, both verbal and nonverbal. When those processes involve more than one cultural or subcultural system, they can be readily confused or misunderstood (Fine, 1982; Kim, 1988). In health care, it is common for interaction to involve making decisions across cultures, or at least to influence such decisions. At times decisions are imposed from one culture onto another. To be cross-culturally effective, however, all interaction and decisions necessitate awareness, sensitivity, knowledge, and skills.

Patterns of similarities and differences between cultural and subcultural groups further reflect social organization and process. Members of social categories share characteristics that distinguish them from members of other social categories. Membership in categories is based primarily on symbolic meaning of classifications. For example, patterned characteristics are used to classify, categorize, or label members of groups. Many characteristics cross classificatory boundaries, while others carry, at least part of the time, significant predictive value. For instance, families that are poor are more likely to be oriented toward the present time than toward the future regarding health (Taylor, 1989). Another example involves traditional Chinese individuals who believe that personality comes from the blood and may, therefore, resist transfusions for that reason (Chien, 1991). Both of these brief examples have numerous implications for communication, presentation, and acceptance of information, as well as for intervention practices related to health maintenance, illness prevention, or health restoration.

Cross- or Transcultural Communication

Contact and interaction between persons who identify themselves as distinct from one another in cultural terms comprise cross-cultural communication (Collier & Thomas, 1988; Pedersen, 1988).

An eclectic definition of culture is used: a learned system of symbols with shared values, meanings, and behavioral norms. Cultural differences involve patterned lifeways, values, beliefs, ideals, and practices. Cultural and subcultural differences are not limited to extreme contrasts (in, for example, language, national origin, or political orientation), but often involve more subtle differences (such as those between religious, class, age, or gender groups). Culture, according to Kim (1988), is conceptualized as applying to all aggregates or categories of people whose "life patterns discernibly influence individual communication behaviors" (pp. 12-13).

The extent of cultural difference present in a given interaction depends on the degree of heterogeneity in the worldviews of those interacting, as well as in their belief systems, overt behaviors, verbal and nonverbal code systems, relationships, and intentions (Sarbaugh, 1988). The adjectives "cross-cultural" and "transcultural" are distinguished from "multicultural" because transcultural or cross-cultural imply a bridging of significant differences in cultural or subcultural communication styles, beliefs, or practices. Multicultural, in contrast, denotes maintenance of several distinct cultural or subcultural forms. A simplistic but useful way to differentiate "cross-" cultural from "multicultural" is to use the analogy of children engaged in playing a game (which implies effective communication and interaction between or "across" children) versus children engaged in parallel play (which refers to several separate and noninteractive activities).

An Interactive Decision Model

To understand communicative processes, it is important to recognize how a specific situation is being handled or transacted. The Interactive Decision Model presented in Figure 1.1 evolved from listening to students and colleagues, as well as each other, attempt to understand interactive situations in health care settings.

Every situation involves behavioral choices, although those may or may not be perceived or considered acceptable. Ideally, problem-solving communication flows from the situation through choices that facilitate direct intervention, respectful engagement, and mutual communication. The Interactive Decision Model illustrates the two-way potential for the flow of communication. Opportunities

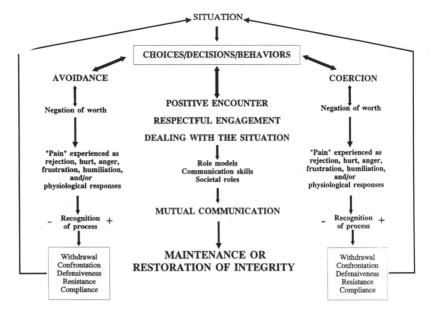

Figure 1.1. Interactive Decision Model

always exist for reassessment of a situation and its accompanying decisions. The bi-directional nature of the process also increases potential for resorting to avoidance or coercion as means of responding to a situation. Responses to decisions constitute a new situation with opportunities for new considerations and choices.

Some decisions lead to more productive outcomes than others, although all decisions effect outcomes of some type. It is proposed here that mutual communication, illustrated by the center portion of the Interactive Decision Model, is the most productive approach in situations involving diversity and cultural variables. This proposition is based on the following premises:

1. Choices, decisions, and behaviors reflect learned beliefs, values, ideals, and preferences.
2. Choices, decisions, and behaviors that are based on a belief in the inherent superiority of one group over another (whether the basis is age, sex, race, national origin, or any other stratifying category) are unjust and untenable. Such attitudes and beliefs constitute prejudice.

Actions based on those attitudes or beliefs are discriminatory (Ritzer et al., 1982).

3. Responses of individuals and groups of individuals tend to become patterned and predictable, although variations and changes can and do occur.

4. The goal, and hoped-for outcome, of mutual communication is maintenance or restoration of personal integrity, which implies a sense of wholeness and recognition of worthiness of respect (that is, of regard, acknowledgment, and visibility).

Respectful engagement or encounter does not imply a negative encounter. Encounter, confrontation, and conflict are not inherently offensive or otherwise negative. Avoidance and "invisibility," that is, the denial of issues, are often more painful than is encounter or direct and effective management of those issues.

Avoidance and Coercion

Situations tend to develop in predictable patterns. Sensitive or controversial issues are often responded to by behaviors that represent avoidance or coercion (or first one and then the other of those). Although they may seem to maintain established patterns, it is a superficial peace. Both avoidance and coercion are stereotyping and dehumanizing interactive patterns.

Avoidance is defined as lack of acknowledgment, whether conscious or unconscious, of an issue or person. It involves remaining unaware, overlooking, and/or not acknowledging characteristics of a situation, including similarities or differences between or among individuals. Situations and/or their participants are treated as if they were invisible or can be ignored. Avoidance also enforces invisibility of the issues and often of those persons associated with the issues by minimizing or denying the existence of traits, contributions, or problems that are part of the life experience of some individuals. Avoidance maintains and perpetuates inequity by perpetuating the status quo and failing to stimulate change.

For example, the hospital administrator who tries to ignore that racial or ethnic issues are problematic among the staff (when indeed they are) is avoiding the issue. Given that scenario, other administrators and managers in the system may desire to encourage or discourage open discussion of issues among the staff, but, for a number of reasons, are unlikely to disregard the hospital administrator's position and example. Open discussion provides an opportunity for mutual communication (whether or not mutual communication occurs), and potentially for change. Avoidance precludes that opportunity. It is, therefore, a powerful and controlling, albeit stultifying, strategy.

Situations do not go away simply because they are ignored or avoided. Aspects of them may eventually surface. If the environment becomes receptive to acknowledgment of the issue or person, visibility may increase. If the situation reaches an intolerable level of desperation, anger, and/or frustration, however, reactions may occur at any point on a continuum that goes from passive acceptance to rage (Thomas & Sillen, 1979; Banton, 1983; Hewitt, 1984; Dyer et al., 1989). A frequently reported response of managers who have avoided a staff issue is, when the issue resurfaces, formulation of policy that coerces its superficial resolution. Insistence that the issue no longer be visible in the environment, however, does not imply its resolution. Various responses are possible. For example, the issue may be propelled underground and anger provoked.

Coercion involves the use of status, power, and/or wealth to compel or persuade people to act in specific ways. Although coercion is not by definition negative, the subtlety of coercive tactics in conjunction with inequity of power often lead to negative consequences. Coercion occurs because of the inequity of power, but not all coercion involves inequity. Consider the difference between limiting a selection of ice cream flavors and a selection of career choices. In either case, coercive tactics limit options and may result in powerlessness, although the significance of the outcome varies greatly.

Power occurs in various forms, such as force, manipulation, and persuasion (Wrong, 1988). Those who possess power are in the best position to determine which issues move from private to public domain (that is, to legitimize issues or problems), to control the definition of issues and problems, to advance their own interests, and to determine what (if anything) is to be done to solve a problem or issue (Neubeck, 1986).

In interactive situations, control through coercion does not emphasize resolution of the situation, but, rather, use of power (Langer, 1983; Martin, 1983; Wendell, 1990). Inequities typically remain, although overt evidence of the situation may temporarily abate. Those who must control their position may be responding to the perception of threat or fear. The use of coercion in a situation may result in anger, which is a normal response to feelings of powerlessness that result from being or feeling controlled (Freidson, 1970; Langer, 1983; Beck, Rawlins, & Williams, 1984; Rathus, 1987; Cross, 1987). In essence, a forced response usually gets an angry response.

Situations tend to be handled by avoidance or coercion (or avoidance *and* coercion) when it is not understood that both passivity and aggression perpetuate the problem by failing to change or resolve the underlying situation (Korda, 1975). Those behavioral responses function to ignore and/or control.

People do not always choose to act in ways that dehumanize; they may not recognize the impact of their actions. It is the subtlety of processes such as avoidance and coercion that makes actions elusive and difficult to change. At times the issue is not identified as real or legitimate due to a lack of awareness or sensitivity. Feelings of powerlessness may also be associated, with avoidance or coercive behaviors resulting from resentment toward the situation, with those that they view as involved, or from being personally involved.

Both avoidance and coercion risk blaming the victim, that is, projecting negativism about the situation (or similar situations) toward the victim rather than toward the cause or root of the problem (Daniels & Kitano, 1970; Terry, 1970, 1981; Bowser & Hunt, 1981; Jones, 1981; Wendell, 1990). Victims, like perpetrators, can be individuals, groups, or institutions.

Definitions

There are a number of additional concepts, the definitions of which are important in the understanding of cultural and social patterns that relate to health, illness and care.

Social Process

Social process refers to patterns of behavior or interaction that express societal expectations, that is, the norms or rules that are learned and followed to get along in a society. Social process involves commonly observed or collective responses. For example, health care providers often, consciously or unconsciously, show deference to males and physicians. Deference is displayed because it has been learned that males and physicians have status, power, and wealth (expressed in this case as income, education, knowledge, and other valued resources) that are superior to the status, power, and wealth of most nonphysicians. Cultural values and social norms are reflected in the expression of deference.

Status

Status or social prestige and the influence that comes with it may be measured in many ways. Those include notoriety, recognition, or deference associated with special social standing. With upward or downward social mobility, status may be gained or lost. Being a social phenomenon, status is always relative to that of others.

Minority or Subordinate Status

Subordinate or minority status refers to social position that is less than that ascribed to members of another group or groups. It is common for customs and values associated with respect to be withheld as a result of limited status, power, and/or wealth. Minority status is usually not an artifact of numbers but, rather, of power (Ritzer et al., 1982; Semmes, 1985). For example, women in the United States outnumber men, but men remain more powerful throughout the society's political, legal, economic, religious, educational, and other institutionalized systems.

People who share certain distinctive physical or cultural characteristics and are subjected to prejudice and discrimination (Wirth, 1938) constitute a minority group. Examples of aggregates of people with limited power, status, and wealth include the aged (Butler, 1969; Steinmetz, 1988), children (Scheper-Hughes, 1987; Boone, 1989), women (Pearce, 1984; Tavris & Wade, 1984), ethnic and racial minorities (Semmes, 1985; U. S. Department of Health and Human Services, 1985; Geller, 1988), the handicapped (Wertlieb, 1985), and the poor (Kuhn & Bluestone, 1987; Wilson, 1987; Winnick, 1988; Maxwell, 1989).

Power

Power is the ability to get people to do things that they otherwise might or would not do. Power is the crucial variable in minority-majority relations and affects the ability of individuals or groups to realize their goals and interests, even in the face of resistance to the power. Members of relatively powerful groups typically recognize less similarity between themselves and members of less powerful groups than vice versa (Foster & White, 1982).

It is important to realize that authority is only one aspect of power. For example, it is possible to have a high-ranking position without the authority or ability to issue and enforce decisions and commands (Wrong, 1988) that allow decisions or changes to be made at that level. There has been considerable concern about the extent to and manner in which health care providers and institutions are or should be agents of social control (Navarro, 1979; Brown, 1980; Foucault, 1980; Turner, 1987).

Empowerment

Empowerment refers, in most cases, to self-direction and self-determination (Dennis, 1991). However, for many peoples a pattern of shared control is expected and appropriate (Dennis, 1990; Degner & Russell, 1988). Whereas power often connotes either personal or impersonal situations, empowerment typically suggests personal control.

Wealth

Wealth is worth measured in terms of economic and valued commodities. Economic worth is known as class. Wealth is measurable in numerous entities (for example, land, employees, livestock, or equipment and material goods). In America and other industrialized societies, wealth usually implies monetary resources.

Institutions

Institutions are relatively permanent patterns of social organization and behavior that exert control and meet societal needs. Examples include marriage, organized religion, educational systems, and stratification by race, sex, or ethnicity.

Self-Fulfilling Prophecy

A self-fulfilling prophecy occurs when a predetermined or expected outcome is acted out. For example, the expectation that mentally retarded adults cannot be productive citizens may result in limitations of opportunities that render members of that population nonproductive. Likewise, the expectation that they are capable of meaningful training and employment has resulted in those outcomes.

Social Categories

As members of society, we have each learned to recognize, characterize, rank for social acceptability or presumed worth, and probably stereotype members of various social categories (Hirschfield, 1984; Aboud & Skerry, 1984). Typically, such classifications represent aggregates of people who share one or more common characteristics, but who neither interact with one another nor gather in one place (Thio, 1986). It is useful to think of social categories as subcultures, that is, as cultures within a culture that are distinguishable by shared and patterned cultural values and social norms that affect (despite individual interpretation and variation) communication, behavioral choices, and experience (Howard, 1986). Members of various health-oriented disciplines or occupational subcultures, for example, share sets of beliefs, values, and rules for getting along that differ from those of other disciplines.

The process of categorization permeates nearly every aspect of our lives. For each of us, subjective experience and exposure to collective classification schemes shape values, beliefs, norms, roles, and attitudes (Brislin et al., 1986). We associate those ideas with ranks and values that we learn as we are socialized into society. Specific positions (statuses) in society are ascribed to or acquired by members of social categories (Linton, 1936). For example, sick roles (Landy, 1977), sex roles, rural or urban background, ethnic group membership, and socioeconomic class imply social categories and statuses. Each status carries with it a set of rules for expected behaviors (that is, a role), as well as a variety of implications regarding its worth or value. The 70-year-old Greek-American is not expected to behave as he or she did when 20; the status has changed and the associated set of behaviors is also expected to change, although some characteristics, such as sex and ethnicity, have not. We each hold many statuses and have numerous roles. The same individual may, for example, be a physical therapist, parent, faculty member, Democrat, friend, scholar, consumer, middle-aged, male, Chinese, sibling, Methodist, diabetic, city dweller, and so on, with each status implying specific role expectations as well as social position. Although individuals interpret their roles differently, social categories are important because their socially ascribed meanings strongly influence individual and group experience.

Health Beliefs and Practices

Every society has a culture, and every cultural group has a system of beliefs and practices that reflects its general worldview but also relates specifically to health and illness (Helman, 1990; Johnson & Sargent, 1990). Success of the human species is at least due in part to the ability to cope with medical problems (Laughlin, 1963) and each society has invested in those concerns with healing specialists, a materia medica, and sets of beliefs that are integrated with the rest of the culture (Lieban, 1974; Singer, 1977; Foster & Anderson, 1978; Romanucci-Ross, Moerman, & Tancredi, 1983; Helman, 1990). Those beliefs and practices change with time and circumstances, but they are generally maintained unless something else supplants them. Immigrants and others may utilize American health care resources with no more change in their original belief systems than might be experienced if one became ill while visiting another country.

Most ideas about health and illness come from everyday experiences in specific biological, psychological, social, and cultural contexts. Likewise, most health care occurs at home and in informal systems of interaction (Helman, 1990). Virtually no one runs for professional help at the first hint of a symptom. Traditional and folk remedies, most of them as benign as herbal tea, might be used and a homemade diagnosis and etiology tentatively constructed. The next resort may be to popular or over-the-counter resources, which may or may not be associated with allopathic medicine. Finally, if relief is not in sight, professional consult is likely to be undertaken. Each phase implies many decisions, however. What a symptom is and what it means, whether to treat it or ignore it, how to treat it, who to go to, when to go, what symbolizes relief or a worsening condition—each is a judgment call, and each analysis will call on past experience and the perception of present options. In a diverse population, such judgments are made with widely varying criteria.

Each of us has a system of explanation in which ideas about the meaning, cause, process, and treatment of illness are put into workable perspective. This conceptual framework, called an explanatory model, involves recognition, identification, disease or illness classification, etiology, prevention, and prognosis (Kleinman, 1980). The explanatory model provides a framework for interpreting cues that alert one to becoming or being ill and determine what is done about it and why, as well as for maintaining health and preventing illness. It is often assumed that consumers share providers' explanatory models, or that all providers share the same one, although neither is expectable in a diverse society.

In modern western societies, explanations for illness are typically rooted in natural phenomena, such as infection with microorganisms, mechanical dysfunctions, or stress. For less scientifically oriented peoples, however, belief systems indicate that illness and disease result from social or supernatural phenomena, such as failing to follow group rules or having invoked the disfavor of powerful mystical or spiritual forces (Helman, 1990; Spector, 1991). To be effective, therapies are expected to match the etiologies (Foster & Anderson, 1978; Helman, 1990). People who believe that the root of disease is spiritual may value prayer or other spiritual interventions over medical intervention. Likewise, groups such as those Native Americans who believe that illness is a social phenomenon (that is, a problem with social interaction) may execute elaborate ritualized ceremonies (such as sings or sand painting) for therapy, rather than intervening directly with the ill patient (Eaton, 1982; Adair, Deuschle, & Barnett, 1988; Hammerschlag, 1988).

Health care professionals associated with the biomedical system do not consistently offer opportunities for clients to discuss their explanatory models or expectations of treatment as they relate to those beliefs. Without knowledge of those perspectives, however, accurate assessment is impaired and effective intervention potentially compromised.

Care

The common commodity among health-related disciplines is care. Care that is acceptable to members of specific groups requires understanding of and respect for life-style, community, and sociocultural orientations as the context for health promotion, maintenance, and restoration (Bauwens, 1978; Brownlee, 1978; Dougherty, 1985; Leininger, 1988b). Care and caring involve meanings, patterns, processes, and methods that affect health behavior and that occur in patterns that are specific to cultural and subcultural groups (Watson, 1988a; Leininger, 1988a). For example, whereas European American clients are likely to value health education, African American clients are more likely to value the involvement and presence of the provider than the knowledge he or she imparts (Leininger, 1985c). Because what constitutes care is population-specific (Leininger, 1988a, 1988b; Boyle & Andrews, 1989), it follows that definition of appropriate caring behaviors is also bound by social categories and cultural expectations.

Care has been variously characterized (Morse, Bottorff, Neander, & Solberg, 1991) as an enabling phenomenon (Leininger, 1988a, 1988b), humanistic and scientific (Watson, 1990), art (Watson, 1990), a natural human trait (Benner & Wrubel, 1989), subjective (Benner & Wrubel, 1989; Gadow, 1989), universal (Ray, 1987a, 1987b, 1989; Leininger, 1988a, 1987b), therapeutic (Leininger, 1984; Larson, 1987), interpersonal (Horner, 1988), and a moral imperative (Watson, 1985, 1988b; Gadow, 1985). It is generally accepted that care is essential for human growth, well-being, coping, curing, and survival (Leininger, 1988b). "Ethnocaring" research approaches have been developed to discover and understand population-specific conceptualizations of care and caring (Leininger, 1981, 1985b; Morse, Solberg, Neander, Bottorff, & Johnson, 1990).

Working in a multicultural society, health care providers in the United States encounter with impressive frequency circumstances that involve more than one subculture or social category. These encounters are confounded by the fact that in American society access to health care is in large part an artifact of membership in social categories (Brown, 1980; Rodwin, 1988), and by a cultural heritage in which patterns of social categorization have often resulted in unequal recognition of the value of individuals, personal freedom and worth, and backgrounds (Weaver & Garrett, 1983).

The importance of understanding diversity is reflected in the implications that the characteristics of social categories have for the provision of care. Recent years have seen a significant shift from a largely unicultural approach in human services to one oriented toward more sensitivity to group, population, or culture-specific needs (Kleinman, 1980; Chrisman & Maretzki, 1982; Hahn & Gaines, 1985; Leininger, 1988b), within which individual consumers require specific products and services (Spradley, 1991).

Culturally congruent care involves decisions and actions that are acceptable and reasonable to the consumer. For care to be acceptable to consumers, it must match their expectations. To match their expectations, it must take into account their worldviews, systems of values and norms, and orientation to health and illness; it must, in other words, be culture specific (Leininger, 1985a, 1985b, 1988a, 1988b). Within that framework, intervention and care may preserve or maintain the client's original cultural perspective and explanatory model, accommodate or negotiate some change while preserving other parts of the original view, or result in restructuring or repatterning of beliefs or behaviors (Leininger, 1988b; Kavanagh, 1991a).

Cultural Relativism

Multiple cultural subsystems (including the religious, philosophical, political, legal, economic, educational, technologic, and others) influence health care systems (Leininger, 1985b). Cultural relativism reflects the idea that various approaches (for example, to health) have merit and are potentially acceptable because each culture or subculture is judged on its own terms and the members' own perceptions, feelings, and rationales (Thio, 1986). A basic premise is that people have reasons for their decisions and behaviors, whether or not they can articulate those reasons or the health care worker recognizes what they are.

Another fundamental idea is that there are always at least two perspectives on every phenomenon: the *emic*, which is the insider's point of view, and the *etic*, which is the outsider's understanding of the situation (Draguns, 1981; Hughes, 1990; Stein, 1990). Think about your own discipline. Physicians may be convinced that they have a more valid view of medicine than a nurse or a psychologist would have because the physician has an insider's, or emic, perspective. Both perspectives involve trade-offs; the emic view provides the subjective experience but limits objectivity, whereas the etic perspective is more objective, but is farther from actual experience of the phenomenon. Because we are each a product of our culture(s), culture provides the filters through which we each interpret reality. Culture, thus, precludes the possibility of truly neutral observation (Farley, 1988). The culturally sensitive health care provider becomes adept at gaining both etic and emic perspectives.

Attempts to grasp an emic perspective protect against ethnocentrism, which refers to being centered in one's own cultural or subcultural orientation to the extent that other perspectives are impeded (Brislin et al., 1986; Kavanagh, 1991a). Using a set of behavioral standards developed according to the norms of one culture to assess a client from another culture is a cultural imposition based on ethnocentricity.

Despite its enabling attributes, the flexibility of cultural relativism can leave health care providers in a quandary. When people from diverse cultural backgrounds interact, it is at times difficult to understand where each culture begins and ends—and, indeed, they often overlap. Therefore, although the concept of cultural relativism tends to be idealized in the social sciences, many health care practitioners find it unsettling. Concern over relativism is often focused on the roles that assessment and judgment play in the provision of care. True relativism implies the lack of a set of absolute values and of criteria by which to decide among the variety of values that exist (Monro, 1973). Normality and abnormality lose their boundaries. Based on what is generally expected or accepted from the perspective of a specific social category, when considered in the context of relativism they become elastic.

Can these worldviews mix (Tax, 1990)? Is there an acceptable middle ground? In the simplest terms, yes, they can and there is—usually. In fact, it is increasingly obvious that the ideal solution in health care is a workable and working coalition somewhere between absolutism and relativism. Conflict-based approaches, whether applied as avoidance or coercion, tend to be neither productive nor appealing.

Constructive multiculturalism draws ideas, customs, histories, and explanatory models together for comparison and sharing of diversity (Finn, 1990). It avoids victimization and separatism. Flexibility is required, however, and that flexibility can be threatening when, for example, as a student you struggled to commit to logic and memory exact rules for differentiating normality from abnormality. You may or may not have given much thought to where those standards came from or that they represent the values and norms of the dominant culture and cannot in most cases be generalized beyond that to others.

Even cultural relativism has its limitations. A naive, blanket acceptance of beliefs and practices as functionally or ethically neutral may be harmful and may lead providers to be inappropriately inactive (Devereux, 1967). On the other hand, prejudgment of attitudes, beliefs, and practices is ethnocentric, unfair, and leads to value judgments and victim blaming (Boyle & Andrews, 1989). Such prejudice finishes analysis of the situation before all the data are in.

Is this a no-win situation that the practitioner faces? No, but it can become complex, particularly when legal, policy, or ethical issues confound or contradict cultural beliefs or values. As clinicians we do have limits. For instance, harmful or abusive behaviors are not tolerable, regardless of their motivations, including tradition. On the other hand, most traditional health beliefs and practices are benign enough to cause no ill harm, unless their use prolongs the decision to seek professional help (Helman, 1990). It is vitally important to assess from the client's perspective what the most appropriate goals are in a given situation. Basically, as previously described, there are three possibilities for culturally appropriate health care: helping to preserve the cultural orientation, negotiating some change in the cultural orientation, or repatterning that original orientation (Leininger, 1988b).

Social Stratification

How differences are perceived and dealt with is central to understanding diversity, social classification, and social stratification

(Rothenberg, 1990). A relativistic approach to analysis of a given situation is useful in understanding social stratification and its consequence, social inequality. The latter implies differential access to resources, unequal life chances or opportunities, the likelihood of devaluation of specified individuals and groups, and numerous social costs (Berreman, 1981; Ritzer et al., 1982; Thio, 1986).

Everyone values status, wealth, and power. Although what constitutes those resources varies widely from society to society, it is their distribution that forms the basis for social stratification. To understand social process in the United States, it is important to note that, despite interrelationships among the three resources, the most eminent seems to be power. Power is the ability to get people to do what is wanted of them, sometimes with disregard of their own preferences or intentions (Berreman, 1981; Thio, 1986; Wrong, 1988). Power is the factor that distinguishes minority from majority status (Ritzer et al., 1982). Consequently, women outnumber men in the United States and blacks outnumber whites in South Africa, but women and blacks are not the majority for they have less power than and are subordinate to the dominant group.

In the health care arena differential access to resources limits basic and preventative health care to members of some groups. Unequal distribution of health care resources results in morbidity and mortality rates that vary substantially with ethnic category and economic class. For example, average life expectancies for European Americans are significantly longer than those of nonwhite populations (Wilson, 1987; Rodwin, 1988; Kramer, 1988; Boone, 1989; Rogers, 1989). Likewise, in the United States babies of poor families, regardless of ethnic or racial background, die at twice the rate of babies of nonpoor families (Boone, 1982, 1989; Scheper-Hughes, 1987; Kramer, 1988). Of the industrialized nations, only the United States and South Africa do not have some type of nationalized health service (Helman, 1990). Although it has often been said that an American system of health care available to everyone would be excessively costly, efforts to reduce expenses in the short run can lead to higher, long-term societal costs for remedial and rehabilitative resources (Wright, 1983; McElroy & Townsend, 1989; Boone, 1989). Nonetheless, the dominant American values, which maintain the present system, hold personal freedom and individual competitiveness to be of greater worth than equality (Navarro, 1979; Brown, 1980; Scheper-Hughes, 1987; Kavanagh, 1991a).

Unequal life chances and opportunities may take many forms, including, for example, anything from overall educational opportunities to discrimination against individuals due to physical appearance. Regarding health care, however, there are strong correlations between access to health care and level of well-being and health. "Access" is not limited to "permission," but also includes acceptability of the services, which influences utilization (Milio, 1971).

The devaluation of specific groups has been a part of America's history and heritage since its inception (Daniels & Kitano, 1970; Bowser & Hunt, 1981; Jones, 1981; Gaines, 1982; McGoldrick, 1982; Monrroy & Orque, 1983; Phinney & Rotheram, 1987; Takaki, 1987; Geller, 1988). It is not surprising that a number of blind spots, many of them built into the dominant system, continue to surface in interactions among members of various American subcultures. As a consequence, however, the health care sector reflects the dominant society. A system of "minority" and "majority" categories results in underrepresentation of members of disadvantaged groups in high (status, wealth, and power) positions and their overrepresentation in low (status, wealth, and power) positions (Ritzer et al, 1982; Weaver & Garrett, 1983).

Social stratification and inequity are touchy topics for many members of a society that idealizes equality but prioritizes personal freedom and is, in reality, highly stratified. Many people believe (or want to believe) that racial, gender, age, or ethnic issues are no longer important, that they have already been resolved, or that they are of concern only to specific populations. For instance, secretaries sometimes do not pass information about women's programs on to their male bosses on the misconception that women's program activities and issues are of interest only to females. The unfortunate outcome is limited support by males in powerful positions of programs that advance equality for women (Kavanagh, 1990).

Another stumbling block, and one related directly to those "built-in blind spots" noted above, is a tendency to make simple, stereotypic associations between different social categories, such as between ethnic category and economic class (Killian, 1981; Wilson, 1984). For instance, members of ethnic minority groups are overrepresented among the poor, but most are not poor. Most poor people in America are of European descent, and there is a substantial nonwhite middle class, despite stereotypes that equate ethnic minority status with economic minority status (Beneria & Stimpson, 1987; Wilson 1987; Jaynes & Williams, 1989).

In less specific terms, generalized preferences by health care providers for clients similar to themselves and who represent societal ideals have long been observed to result in significant differences in distribution of resources between the "YAVIS" (which stands for young, attractive, verbal, intelligent, and [potentially] successful) (Schofield, 1964; Sue, 1981) and the "QUOIDS" (who are viewed as quiet, unattractive, old, indigent, dissimilar, and stupid) (Pedersen, 1979, 1981).

The costs of social stratification and social inequality extend to all involved in those processes, including members of the majority populations (Bowser & Hunt, 1981; Phinney & Rotheram, 1987). At the very least, self esteem is threatened (Sennett & Cobb, 1973; Mecca et al., 1989) and the integrity of both the majority and minority groups is undermined (Bowser & Hunt, 1981). Self respect is damaged when members of minority or subordinate categories begin to believe in their own inferiority, feel invisible, or feel that they are inconsequential (Lieb, 1978; Fine, 1982; Kumin, 1983). Relationships remain underdeveloped due to social distancing, avoidance, or rejection. Potential is thwarted rather than developed and useful interdependence denied. Last and hardly least, inequity has a divisive impact on society.

Affirmation of diversity involves recognition of the effects of differences, similarities, and social processes on lives. In an ideal world perhaps those phenomena could or would be ignored. In the real world they must be acknowledged as long as they have an impact on the life experiences of individuals.

Professional Responsibility

Attitudes toward diversity are systematically, overtly, and covertly communicated and perpetuated through processes of socialization, education, and interaction (Ritzer et al. 1982; van Dijk, 1987). Educators are in positions to actively interpret and reformulate models of belief, social knowledge, and ideologies held by the society at large (van Dijk, 1987). As scholars and as clinicians, we have the instruments and skills to study and criticize. We are, therefore, individually and collectively responsible for developing the ability to examine and understand our roles in communicating ideas (Sedlacek & Brooks, 1976; Strauss, 1984; Nolde & Smillie, 1987; Regan & Sedlacek, 1989; Stanford University, 1989; Quality Education for Minorities Project, 1990; Kolodny, 1991).

It has been recognized for some years that the cultural relevance of health care and/or education has a profound effect on its reception and utilization. Underutilization is especially pronounced among members of ethnic minority groups (Pedersen, 1981). Evaluation studies have demonstrated that large proportions (in some cases, nearly half) of all ethnic minority clients do not return after one visit (Andrulis, 1977; Ogbu, 1988). Similar findings have been noted by practitioners (Zola, 1981; Lefley, 1984; Liu & Yu, 1985) and educators (Fernandez & Velez, 1985; Neubeck, 1986; Pedersen, 1988; Tollett, 1989; Quality Education for Minorities Project, 1990; Dressler, 1991).

An increasing number of states (including California, Minnesota, North Carolina, and Pennsylvania, among others) now require that teachers become multiculturally prepared (Pedersen, 1988). The question has been asked whether health care practitioners are in any way less responsible for provision of culturally appropriate care (Kleinman, 1977, 1980; Pedersen, 1988; Sedlacek, 1988; Leininger, 1989, 1991). It is anticipated that legal requirements will eventually demand demonstration of understanding of the contributions and life-styles of members of various racial, cultural, and economic groups in society; of recognition of and the ability to cope with dehumanizing biases, discrimination, and prejudices; of creation of learning environments that contribute to self esteem of all persons and to positive interpersonal relations; and of respect for human diversity and personal rights (Pedersen, 1988; Leininger, 1989). The United States' past and present have been shaped by relationships between and among members of social categories. American society is increasingly (if inconsistently) aware of the utility of understanding its diversity. Although rules may require educators to become knowledgeable about multicultural populations in order to teach, culture is only one aspect of diversity. Furthermore course content and professional positions sometimes focus on avoidance of insult in lieu of promotion of understanding and diversity. Because health care providers learn primarily through role modeling (Kendell, 1975; Dougherty, 1985; Bidwell & Brasler, 1989; Helman, 1990), it is important that practitioners and members of faculties as well as students be prepared to facilitate effective handling of intercultural situations, whether encountered in the classroom, the clinical setting, or other aspects of life.

There are more people who do not systematically resist diversity, are not prejudiced, or do not discriminate than there are who do (van Dijk, 1987). Many individuals who are not personally prejudicial or individually discriminatory, however, contribute to social distancing and discriminatory situations because they avoid communication, do not recognize how others interpret their behavior, or fail to prevent inequity (Thomas & Sillen, 1979; Hines & Boyd-Franklin, 1982; Sigelman & Welch, 1991). By not realizing that their behaviors conflict with the values and norms of other groups of people, they inadvertently create social barriers or negate the worth of others (Hamill, 1988).

Discrimination not only reflects prejudicial attitudes of individuals, but also is built into (that is, institutionalized in) society and perpetuated in societal organization and processes (Pinderhughes, 1982; Thio, 1986; Geller, 1988; Wacquant & Wilson, 1989), including the health care system (Weaver & Garrett, 1983; Rodwin, 1988). For example, women are more likely than men to be socialized to be satisfied with jobs rather than careers and with work that promises relatively little upward mobility (Freeman, 1984; Tavris & Wade, 1984; Kuhn & Bluestone, 1987). Because concerted effort is required to cause change in institutionalized societal patterns, inactivity does not prevent or avoid discrimination, but, rather, maintains it as part of the social system.

Summary

Part I of *Promoting Cultural Diversity: Strategies for Health Care Professionals* introduced rationales for commitment to understanding social process and cultural diversity. Background conceptual material is provided for use in the development of awareness, sensitivity, knowledge, and skills related to the management of health care for diverse populations. Information on patterns of social interaction, process, hierarchy and stratification, and a selection of concepts and definitions are discussed to form the foundation for emphasis on respectful engagement and mutual communication.

Questions for Discussion

1. In what ways do health-related problems vary with the culture or subculture of clients and patients?
2. Why are some communication styles more effective than others in working with persons from other backgrounds?
3. How might we learn from other cultures in sharpening our skills as health care providers?
4. What evidence is there that members of health care disciplines are culturally conditioned in their responses?
5. How would you describe the values that generally characterize the predominant American culture?
6. What are the implications of a "self-fulfilling prophecy" for health care providers working with individuals within a multicultural population?
7. What are some of the ways that education programs for health care professionals could be modified to make them more sensitive to value systems in a multicultural society?
8. To what extent is all health care cross-cultural?
9. What are the pros and cons of requiring cross-cultural preparation for health care providers?
10. How should/would/could such preparation, if required, be effectively implemented and evaluated?
11. What aspects of social process have particular impact on communication between members of groups that represent different social categories?
12. How much and what type of preparation for effective cross-cultural communication and intervention should be included in health education, whether or not it is required?

Myths for Discussion

1. It is a myth that educated and professional individuals do not have minority status problems or involve themselves in such issues.

2. It is a myth that personal concern with social stratification issues implies immaturity and a nonprofessional attitude.
3. It is a myth that minorities must adapt to social institutions, rather than institutions adapt to needs of minority groups or individuals.
4. It is a myth that you can "get the feel" or "sense" of another culture without having to learn about its social organization and social processes.
5. It is a myth that health care providers cannot be reasonably prepared to handle cross-cultural and other situations involving diversity because health care personnel in the United States deal with people from more than 100 ethnic, racial, and cultural groups.

Notes on the Myths

1. It is a myth that educated and professional individuals do not have minority status problems or involve themselves in such issues.

The Interaction Decision Model (Figure 1.1) depicts the risks of avoidance and coercion, with which members of any group may be involved. There is no immunity for professionals; nor is it gained with professional education and training. Minority status is determined by who has and who does not have power. Membership in occupational and professional groups does not imply equality with members of the same or other groups. Experiences of health care providers who are members of ethnic minority groups, like members of any other social category, reflect those of ethnic minority group members throughout society (Jackson, 1979; Parreno, 1983).

2. It is a myth that personal concern with social stratification issues implies immaturity and a nonprofessional attitude.

Some categories of social stratification are not based on achievement, contribution, or competence of individuals, but, rather, on historical and interactive tradition. Despite serious lack of evidence that sex, race, ethnicity, or age significantly affect ability to do a job, stereotypes remain and are acted upon. Those stereotypes affect the real-life experience of professionals as well as nonprofessionals. Although professional objectivity and demeanor influence when and how issues are presented, it is unrealistic as well as irresponsible to assume that social stratification issues are irrelevant to health care workers or inappropriate for open discussion (Bowman & Culpepper,

1974; Lieb, 1978; Greenleaf, 1980; Lovell, 1981; Roberts, 1983; Chinn & Wheeler, 1985; Katzman & Roberts, 1988).

Issues involving social distance and unequal access to basic resources (that is, status, power, and wealth) influence work- and non-work-related behaviors. Employment situations are often stratified and inequitable settings. To deny the possibility and/or impact of differential opportunity and experience risks "blaming the victim."

3. *It is a myth that minorities must adapt to social institutions, rather than institutions adapt to needs of minority groups or individuals.*

Many health care personnel expect clients to adapt to the system that is provided. Efficiency, which is valued in the United States (whether the motive is profit, the work ethic, or something else), is facilitated by routinization. In a complex and diverse society such as ours, it is impossible to understand or know all that is relevant to culturally congruent care and treatment. A combination of those two rationales is commonly used in attempts to justify provision of health care characterized by minimal individualization and imposition of the values and norms of America's dominant (that is, Eurocentric, middle class, male, and Christian) society. The fact that large portions of the population represent different sets of health beliefs, practices, assumptions, and theories has not motivated most health care providers to customize care for those peoples. Members of health care disciplines have, for the most part, accepted the assumption that generalized models of care with minor adjustments for individual needs suffice, although that approach denies significant cultural and subcultural variation in health needs, expectations, and responses.

Quality health care, and in particular culturally congruent care, like increased attention to other specific needs, is time dependent (Masson, 1985). A common argument for routinizing health care is the time needed to individualize care. It is hard to imagine medicine agreeing to loss of its tools (surgeons, for example, giving up operating suites or radiologists their equipment), but nurses and others have often accepted expectations that they accomplish more tasks with less time. Although the time needed to provide quality care is probably adequate for skillful provision of culturally appropriate care, health care industries frequently settle into patterns of trying to mass produce "individualized" care. Adequate time for the appropriate provision of care will have to be demanded either by consumers or providers, or both.

The biomedical (allopathic) system developed in response to the need to maintain a large and effective work force (Brown, 1980). Oriented toward pathology, it specialized in diagnosis and treatment, not prevention or rehabilitation. Still a privilege of those (usually members of the productive middle class) who qualify for its services, American health care systems have not generally needed to nor have they been motivated to tailor their services to the needs of specific populations. They remain essentially medicocentric (Kleinman 1978; Pfifferling, 1981). What would it take to create a system to meet the needs of a diverse population?

4. *It is a myth that you can "get the feel" or "sense" of another culture without having to learn about its social organization and social processes.*

Empathic communicators are frequently able to communicate, at least superficially, across significant social, cultural, or physical barriers. If they lack awareness, sensitivity, knowledge, or skills, however, they will be unsuccessful at effecting appropriate interventions.

We all know people who are sensitive to issues or problems that make them feel helpless because they do not know what to do about them. After awhile they may avoid those painful situations and ignore or deny the problems. We also know people who are knowledgeable, but who are not very astute or sensitive about when or how to apply their information. Perhaps even more common are those who are both sensitive and knowledgeable, but who lack the skills that enable effective intervention. Health care providers who fall into that category may, over time, defend themselves by dulling their observations and perspectives to control the sense of powerlessness that comes with the inability to effectively intervene.

Another aspect of this myth involves the fact that most health care disciplines have traditionally focused on individuals. It is probably safe to say that groups of diseases have been studied more often than groups of people. When we work with groups, we often conceptualize them as collections of individuals, failing to see the pattern presented by the group at large. (The old adage "can't see the forest for the trees" comes to mind.) Knowledge of patterns among health-related belief and practice systems, which characterize various groups of people, however, empower health care providers with valuable knowledge for intervention. Verifying individual interpretation within a framework of patterned expectation is far simpler than rediscovering each individual's overall perspective. Continuously "reinventing the wheel" limits progress.

5. *It is a myth that health care providers cannot be reasonably prepared to handle cross-cultural and other situations involving diversity because health care personnel in the United States deal with people from more than 100 ethnic, racial, and cultural groups.*

Some people assume that the fact that health care providers in the United States deal with people from dozens of ethnic, racial, and cultural groups makes it unreasonable to expect them to be ready to provide culturally appropriate and acceptable care. It is indeed unreasonable to expect anyone to know everything about even one group. Complete knowledge is not the goal. Cultural change and individual variation within cultural and subcultural groups reinforce the impracticality of attempting to become "expert" about more than a few groups. On the other hand, general knowledge about cultural patterns and social organization provides a framework for questions and information pertaining to specific groups. Access to this background information provides tools that are valuable to every aspect of the provision of health care.

There is evidence that expectations for culturally congruent care may become as legally binding as are expectations for culturally congruent medical treatment. Just as medical practitioners without informed consent cannot provide treatment without risk of litigation, they and other health care providers are projected to be held responsible in the future for provision of care that is both appropriate by professional standards and acceptable by consumer standards. With between one third and one half of the United States' population representing cultural and subcultural categories that differ significantly from predominant European American, middle-class society, expectations for and standards of acceptable care also vary widely.

Part II   Communication, Intervention, and Diversity

Introduction

Communication is frequently the first challenge when one considers health care that involves diversity. Part II of *Promoting Cultural Diversity: Strategies for Health Care Professionals* provides a repertoire of intervention modes and communication skill areas for use in situations that involve diversity.

Learning takes place as a result of what is done with information (Hyman & Rosoff, 1984). Recognition of care alternatives, development of confidence in cross-cultural communication skills, and the ability to analyze situations in specific terms require practice. To become comfortable with the skills required for effective interaction in situations involving diversity, practice of those skills is of primary importance. Case studies, questions, discussion of myths, simulation, role play, and visuals encourage participants to examine their own and others' beliefs and values as a basis for understanding and respecting diversity (Gorrie, 1989). Numerous teaching-learning

AUTHOR'S NOTE: Rosemary Polomano, University of Maryland School of Nursing, is acknowledged for her contributions to the case study concerning the Hispanic family dealing with a hospitalized, cancer-stricken family member.

strategies are provided in Part II to provide participants with experiences that safely mimic interactions involving diversity.

Intervention and Diversity

Cross-cultural communication skills enable problem-solving processes that are acceptable and appropriate to the client, that is, are culturally congruent (Leininger, 1978). These lead to three possible modes of intervention: care oriented toward cultural preservation, cultural negotiation, or cultural repatterning (Leininger, 1988b).

Cultural Preservation or Maintenance

Care that emphasizes cultural preservation or maintenance facilitates the inclusion or incorporation of helpful and/or harmless health and illness-related beliefs and practices from folk medical systems in biomedical treatment programs. For instance, continuing the traditional use of herbal teas or ethnic foods may encourage acceptance of less familiar aspects of care or treatment plans, as well as assist with meeting hydration and nutritional requirements.

The need for cultural maintenance or preservation was demonstrated by a student who wore an asafetida bag (Spector, 1991) around her neck to ward off contagious disease. Neither attractive nor particularly aromatic, this ubiquitous item caused considerable comment from classmates and left faculty worried that it would result in social isolation for its wearer. Eventually, the student explained that the bag meant far more to her than the prevention of disease. She had recently arrived on a metropolitan campus from a distant rural area and felt generally threatened by the environment. The garlic, other herbs, and bits of dried meat in the bag reminded her of home. The well-meaning admonitions with which she had been sent to the city to take care of herself started with the asafetida bag from home to protect against infectious disease and injury. It did no harm, the student pointed out, and made her feel better. The faculty member agreed.

Cultural Negotiation or Accommodation

Care oriented toward cultural negotiation or accommodation results from identified needs that include both the biomedical and traditional folk medical systems. For example, an elderly hospitalized Japanese man became upset and uncooperative because his bed was situated in the direction used to lay out the deceased in traditional Japan. Simple accommodation of his need for a bed that was positioned differently allayed his fears and allowed him to continue his recuperative progress.

Another example of the need for cultural negotiation or accommodation was demonstrated when an Hispanic family, whose teenage son was being cared for on an oncology unit, persisted in "not complying" (as the health team put it) with the team's instructions when the patient spent Saturdays with the family away from the hospital.

The health care team generally disapproved of the food that the family allowed the boy to eat, their failure to return him to the unit on time for his medication, and general disregard for his therapeutic regimen. This conflict persisted until a physician threatened to not allow the family to take the identified client off the unit and another made derogatory remarks about their level of intelligence.

A meeting was called between the family and the staff to discuss goals and strategies that might foster understanding between both groups. It quickly became clear that to the family, family was everything. They understood that their son/brother probably had a limited time to live, and they wanted to make the most of that time together. The medical team, on the other hand, also understood the life-threatening situation that the young man was in, but sought to prolong that time with nearly any possible means. The two groups had differing values and goals and were working toward different and, at times, conflicting, ends.

The clinical nurse specialist, trained in transcultural nursing, was able to help the staff understand the family's perspective and needs. The staff began to support the family outings rather than oppose them. The family made a greater effort to return the patient to the unit in time for his evening treatment and medications. The staff made a greater effort to understand and communicate respect for the family's perspective.

Cultural Repatterning or Restructuring

At times the repatterning or restructuring of lifeways toward new or different models is indicated (Leininger, 1988b). To be acceptable and accepted, however, it is critical that the changes be meaningful and satisfying to the client. Such instances might involve situations of neglect or abuse or those with severe legal implications. Abuse is not limited to specific ethnic or socioeconomic patterns (Hirschi, 1983; Stark, 1984; Andersen, 1985; Neubeck, 1986; Levinson, 1989); and among families in which abuse occurs, patterns of communication, parenting related to discipline, or other behaviors may need to be restructured to ensure disruption of abusive cycles between generations. Parents may have to be taught, for instance, not to respond to violence with violence.

Quite a different situation calling for a change or divergence from the original cultural perspective was presented by a young immigrant couple. They kept their nine-year-old child home from school to care for two younger children while they worked. A culturally sensitive social worker was able to help them find acceptable low-cost child care and to convince them that it was important that the child go to school. Within a short time the couple, which had resisted the change, was gratified to find that their child excelled there.

Intervention Goals

Whether the outcome is cultural preservation, accommodation, or change, the goal is that the outcomes of intervention be acceptable, meaningful, and satisfying to the client (Leininger, 1988b).

Communication to Affirm Diversity

With survival dependent on social interdependence and interaction, members of various social categories are important to each individual. Typically, interactions are based on response styles and patterns that have worked in the past. When the familiar interaction patterns do not work, individual coping strategies are called into play. A series of decisions follows and are the basis of subsequent behavioral and verbal responses. Those who observe or participate in the responses assign meaning to them. Often those meanings, including those with negative overtones, are not validated with their sources. However, ultimately, behavioral and verbal responses indicate the extent to which differences are respected.

Learning to accept and respect differences between and among people is a dimension of all interpersonal relationships (Brislin & Pedersen, 1976). A major theme of this book is that interactions that involve experiences of negative self worth can be minimized and in many instances avoided. With trust and willingness to engage in risk-taking, one can become adept at making interactions work.

Communication styles vary widely. Culturally appropriate work with traditional Native Americans, for example, often involves extensive periods of silence and nondirective techniques (Richardson, 1981). Those techniques are seldom used by Eurocentric practitioners who are not aware of them, sensitive to their appropriateness, knowledgeable about their content and process, or skillful in their use. Practitioners may be uncomfortable with them due to lack of familiarity or socialization to conflicting communication styles. Smooth and effective communication requires practice, and that involves giving oneself permission to practice, to risk making mistakes, and to try new techniques. The alternative is risk of the loss of clients or nonproductive interactions with them (Sue, 1981; Pedersen, 1988).

The decision to learn to communicate across cultures, that is, with people whose social characteristics differ significantly from one's own, begins with the intent to learn to understand, as much as is possible, across cultural differences. Such efforts are not without reward and enable both pleasurable communication and a basis for analysis, understanding, and development of strategies for effective intervention.

Effective interaction with members of culturally different populations may require communication styles that differ substantially from those that are commonly associated with the middle-class European-Americans who generally represent the health care disciplines and the values that predominate within them. The verbal and nonverbal responses of individuals in differing social, political, and economic circumstances are guided by learned beliefs and norms about what is acceptable and expectable in those settings. Individuals also use value systems from multiple subcultures.

Because it was not necessary for the learning of values to occur within a conscious or an overtly organized context, interactive responses tend to be insidious and to become automatic. There is often limited impetus to question the appropriateness of responses unless problems are encountered during an interaction. Nevertheless, choices are made about how to interact. Responses that have worked in the past are likely to be applied. As discussed previously in reference to the Interactive Decision Model (Figure 1.1), options may include attempts at mutual communication or avoidant or coercive strategies.

Awareness and Sensitivity

Awareness and sensitivity are requisites to effective cross-cultural communication. Awareness involves recognition of issues that relate to interactive processes. Cues to the presence of issues occur on multiple levels, with many being subtle or covert. Sensitivity implies understanding the implications and meanings of the processes from the point(s) of view of those directly affected, that is, from the insider's (or emic) perspective. Cultural sensitivity involves learning new information (Pedersen, 1988) so that various perspectives can be understood and appreciated.

The aware clinician realizes, for example, that sex roles tend to vary with ethnicity. The sensitive clinician recognizes the potential importance of the cue when a question directed to a female client is referred to her husband, father, son, or other male relative for an answer. The specific meaning of the cue for the particular family is not yet known, but the culturally aware and sensitive clinician is appropriately prepared to collect additional information to facilitate understanding of the situation from this client's point of view.

Even among familiar groups (for example, within families and in significant relationships), intracultural differences may be misunderstood and rejected without reconciliation of differences in beliefs and values. There is no reason to believe that explanatory models are always shared or that misinterpretations do not occur in significant relationships as well as among acquaintances and strangers. Errors in interpretation of behavior are particularly likely to occur between those who differ in appearance, life-style, and communication style.

Cultural awareness and sensitivity also imply learning to recognize when old information no longer applies (Pedersen, 1988). For instance, the culturally aware and sensitive AIDS counselor understands that encouraging the use of condoms by members of some African-American communities may be interpreted as a strategy to promote black genocide by limiting reproduction. Therefore the value of condoms in reducing risk of HIV infection must be put into a context that is acceptable to the clients.

Knowledge

Whereas sensitivity and awareness allow empathy, knowledge promotes understanding. Knowledge of social process is essential to understanding intercultural issues. Most of us have experienced situations in which we were aware of and sensitive to differences but lacked specific knowledge and a framework that would help to understand the experience.

Patterns of social interaction, social organization, distribution of resources, and social change are directly relevant to social experience. Much of what is attributed to individual behavior actually reflects the influence of social factors that shape or limit behavioral options. For example, although individual effort and competence are components in the distribution of resources, patterns of actual access to status, power, and wealth also vary with social characteristics such as gender, age, and appearance. Consequently knowledge of social organization is necessary to understand, for example, the low pay ceilings encountered by many women who are employed in predominantly female occupations (Freeman, 1984; Tavris & Wade, 1984; McLanahan & Garfinkel, 1989). Despite decreased sex-role stereotyping in employment, women overall continue to earn significantly less than do men, even when they have equivalent educations, job experience, and job responsibilities (Milkman, 1987; Beneria & Stimpson, 1987). Whereas knowledge of the situation allows its understanding and intervention at the individual and/or societal level, lack of knowledge may lead to blaming the victim for failure to achieve, for being passive, or for other factors resulting at least in part from societal-level processes.

Cultural Communication Skills

Awareness, sensitivity, and knowledge are not sufficient for successful cross-cultural intervention. Transcultural or cross-cultural skills are also necessary. Consider a situation in which you understood clearly what was going on, but you did not know what to do about it. Cross-cultural communication skills build upon awareness, sensitivity, and knowledge to allow effective intervention (Pedersen et al., 1981; Pedersen, 1988). Effective cross-cultural communication requires awareness that communication is possible and that mistakes will occur, sensitivity to the communication process, knowledge of expectable patterns of communication styles that are appropriate to the client, and a set of practiced skills.

There are four cross-cultural communication skill areas (Pedersen, 1988). The first is the ability to articulate and present an issue or problem as it is perceived from another's perspective. The utility of this skill is obvious as health care providers are frequently in positions to help clients communicate to others who might misinterpret, misunderstand, or impose their own perspectives on the client. Advocacy often involves articulation of a problem or issue from another's point of view to decrease the risk of imposition of values and norms that are not those of the client.

The second and third skill areas involve recognizing and reducing resistance and defensiveness. Forming the basis of pejorative attitudes and negative labels such as "noncompliance," resistance and defensiveness directly impede development of productive relationships between health care providers and consumers. The trick to developing skills to decrease resistance or defensiveness is recognition of specific ways in which they are displayed. Sensitivity to only generalized forms of these phenomena does not facilitate doing something about them.

The fourth cross-cultural communication skill area involves acknowledgment that we all make interactive mistakes and that taking the risk of making an error is preferable to playing it safe and not communicating (which in itself also communicates). Communication recovery skills (Pedersen, 1988) supply reclamation techniques to use after a blunder.

Communicating across cultures requires the ongoing testing of stereotypes against reality and the modification of interaction according to the evidence (Pedersen, 1988). For example, the assumption that grammatical errors reflect limited intelligence or educational deficits may mislead assessment if it is not recognized that speech patterns also reflect social change or adjustment (perhaps associated with language differences), or may otherwise be independent of the capacity to understand. Speaking style is also sometimes used to create boundaries (just as jargon does among occupational groups), to indicate group membership, or to test others. In essence, the process of communicating generates "in-groups" and "out-groups." The skilled communicator learns how to bridge those differences.

Diversity, Interactive Patterns, and Mutual Communication

In health care the goal of respectful engagement, interaction, and mutual communication is effective and appropriate intervention, which implies being acceptable to the client as well as to the health care professional. Often this is most challenging in situations that are emotional or are considered "sensitive" or touchy by the participants. It may be those circumstances in which respectful and mutual exchange are most needed, yet, due to the discomfort and defensiveness they generate, the circumstances inhibit involvement if they are not adeptly and assertively managed.

Mutual communication conveys commitment to involvement in interactive processes with respect and with the intent of avoiding barriers to mutual exchange. The goal of mutual communication is maintenance or restoration of the integrity of individuals or groups. Such an encounter is mutual in goal and process. Commitment to mutual communication is based on four assumptions:

1. The recognition and value of human dignity,
2. Cultural relativism as an acceptable and preferred condition,
3. Willingness to alter personal behavior in response to the communication process, and
4. Willingness to decrease personal resistance and defensiveness.

Discerning Communicative Patterns

It takes skill to examine communication patterns and their potential for creating either communicative barriers or mutually respectful interactions. Numerous social processes complicate or facilitate the analytical process. Consider the following examples and observations:

1. Social status and hierarchy (for example, among medical, nursing, other disciplines, auxiliary personnel, and client populations

in health care settings) have impact on communication (Britain & Cohen, 1980).

2. Humor is at times the vehicle most comfortably utilized for communication from lower-ranked persons to upper-ranked persons. More direct communication may be viewed as impertinent or otherwise insubordinate. Humor related to some topics (for instance, race or ethnicity) is frequently considered socially unacceptable.

3. Communication often flows primarily downward from hierarchical superior to subordinate. Relations between medical and nursing personnel, for example, traditionally emphasized medicine's instructions (that is, orders) for nursing and less often encouraged serious consideration of nursing feedback by medical personnel (Kavanagh, 1988, 1991b).

4. Hierarchical superiors may know significantly less about their subordinates than vice versa (Berreman, 1962). Does your boss, advisor, or landlord know as much about you as you think you know about him or her? It is often to the advantage of the subordinate individual to have more extensive and more current information about his or her superior than vice versa. Typically, subordinate persons learn as much as possible about their hierarchical superiors to maximize opportunities for survival and advancement. Those with power and authority may not be motivated to get to know those on whom they do not depend for approval.

5. Hierarchical superiors are less likely to experience minority status (as gender minorities, ethnic minorities, occupational minorities, etc.) than are individuals in lower-level situations. This is in part why they often know less about their subordinates, although many persons in hierarchically superior positions are interested in their subordinates for professional reasons related to effective management or goal accomplishment. However, they may or may not examine closely the role that status differences play in their relationships.

6. Clients may be expected to follow different interactive rules than those used by professionals. A commonplace example is the practice by which clients are addressed by first names, and staff (in particular, physicians) are addressed by title or by title and surname. Consider, too, common patterns of who may interrupt whom, who initiates and terminates conversations, who waits for whom, patterns of turn taking, and control over when clients come and go. How mutually distributed is control over behavior and access to resources? A double set of standards is especially noticeable when clients who are seriously ill, mentally ill, or of different

national origin or social class than the provider are not expected to demonstrate the typical norms of interaction or common decency (Kavanagh, 1988, 1991b). While staff may at times be expected to perform at unrealistically high behavioral standards, patients or clients may be expected to behave in socially unacceptable ways.

7. Double standards may be maintained in relationships with hierarchical superiors. It may be viewed, for example, as acceptable for hierarchical superiors but not subordinates to criticize administrative behaviors or procedures.

What other patterns of communication have you observed?

Strategies to Encourage Mutual Communication

Trust, genuineness, and empathy are the bases of all effective communication and rapport (Truax & Carkhuff, 1967). Despite significant differences in patterns of self-disclosure, eye contact, stance, gestures, language, and listening styles (Flaskerud, 1989), all individuals and groups desire respect. Mutual and shared understanding is the goal. Cultural barriers, however, may limit mutuality in health care relationships (for example, when clients depend upon health care providers as experts and decision makers). Effective handling of social differences requires full and free communication, regardless of rank and power (Terry, 1970).

Respectful engagement is facilitated by development of specific skill areas, such as articulating the problem, managing resistance and defensiveness, and recovering when mistakes are made (Ivey, 1980; Pedersen, 1988). Such skills empower or enable the communicator professionally and personally. Respectful engagement and mutual communication, in turn, are the media of social change (Damon, 1989).

The Process of Mutual Communication

Mutual communication involves awareness and knowledge of social process and sensitivity to and recognition of communicative and other barriers. Awareness of the meaning of any experience of others from the other's (or others') point of view is crucial. The effective communicator learns to acquire and to understand, to the greatest extent possible, both insider (emic) and outsider (etic) perspectives.

Tolerance and acceptance of others' attitudes, beliefs, and behaviors, and the willingness to expose oneself as limited and still developing sensitivity, knowledge, and skills are important strategies. Most important is the ability to empathize, that is, to understand others' beliefs, assumptions, perspectives, and feelings (Pedersen, 1988).

General goals recommended by the authors to facilitate communication among members of diverse groups include (Kavanagh, 1991a, p. 198):

1. Promote a feeling of acceptance.
2. To the extent possible, establish open communication.
3. Present yourself with confidence; shake hands if it is appropriate.
4. Strive to gain the other's trust, but do not resent it if you do not get it.
5. Understand what members of the cultural or subcultural group consider as "caring," both attitudinally and behaviorally.
6. Understand the relationship between the other and authority.
7. Understand the other's desire to please and his or her motivation to comply or not to comply.
8. Anticipate diversity, and avoid stereotypes by sex, age, ethnicity, socioeconomic status, and other social categories.
9. Avoid assumptions about where people come from; let them tell you instead. (Most people are pleased when others show sincere interest in them.)
10. Understand the other's goals and expectations.
11. Make your goals realistic.
12. Emphasize positive points and strengths of health beliefs and practices.
13. Show respect, especially for males, even if it is females or children you are interested in. (Males are often decision makers about follow-up.)
14. Be prepared for the fact that children go everywhere with members of some cultural groups as well as with families who do not have options due to economic limitations. Include them.
15. Know the traditional, health-related practices common to the group with whom you are working, and do not discredit any of them unless you *know* specific practices are harmful.
16. Know the folk illnesses and remedies common to the group with whom you are working, and do not discredit them unless you *know* they are harmful.

17. Try to make the setting comfortable; consider colors, music, atmo-sphere, scheduling expectations, seating arrangements, pace, tone, and other environmental variables.
18. Whenever possible and appropriate, involve the leaders of the local group. (Confidentiality is important, but the leaders know the problems and often can suggest acceptable interventions.)
19. Respect values, beliefs, rights, and practices although some may con-flict with your own or with your determination to make changes. (Every group and individual wants respect above all else.)
20. Learn to appreciate the richness of diversity as an asset rather than as a hindrance to communication and effective intervention.

Outcomes of Mutual Communication

Membership in social categories by gender, age, occupation, ethnic-ity, or negatively stigmatized conditions influences experience and worldviews. Outcomes of mutual communication involve empow-erment through awareness of one's own values, others' perspec-tives, and the ability to make effective choices. Mutual, cross-cultural communication facilitates coping with change and appreciation of alternatives. It also fosters recognition of bias resulting from culture-bound, time-bound, or class-bound worldviews. In sum, mutual com-munication promotes the ability to help clients and others to find and accept appropriate intervention.

Communication Role Models

Positive role models are crucial to mutual communication and effective encounters. Because every peer and collegial relationship has the potential for significant role modeling, the roles of instructors, supervisors, upper-division students, and advisors are integral. However, it is often hierarchical situations that are most noticed and subordinates tend to follow the example of hierarchical superiors in handling issues involving diversity. Therefore it is particularly im-portant that persons in positions of authority—as are health care professionals—be aware of, sensitive to, knowledgeable about, and skillful in those situations. Somewhat ironically, due to patterns and practices that commonly result in tracking of minority individuals into subordinate positions and minimal training of supervisory personnel in effective management of diversity, it often happens that those in the most visible and authoritative statuses are not the most prepared to role model effective attitudes regarding diversity or cross-cultural communication skills. It is also common for members of ethnic minority groups to feel that they must deny their own minority orientations due to others' minimization of the importance of that status in their lives (Kavanagh, 1988, 1991b).

On the other hand, individuals in subordinate positions may perpetuate their own powerlessness and minority status positions by following the example of those who are not aware of, sensitive to, knowledgeable about, or skillful in handling diversity. Aged persons, for instance, may resolve themselves to dependent, nonproductive lives due to societal expectation rather than to diminished capacity.

Barriers and Resistance to Communication

Students often ask why attention to cultural diversity is not more prominent in their occupational preparation. In the practice arena, it is no less common to encounter resistance to the effort that is required to communicate and to provide care that is appropriate and acceptable to diverse clients. Such resistance can and should be anticipated, in particular when situations involve unfamiliar, cross-cultural, or complex inequitable circumstances. Health care providers who affirm diversity, however, facilitate health care across cultures. As role models they may find it frustrating to work with others who do not value such endeavors. A brief discussion of the forms that resistance takes and its recognition is indicated. Although resistance is typically attributed to the client (and most notably to that client with that seemingly ubiquitous label, "noncompliant"), it is the provider that we emphasize here.

Numerous excuses and rationalizations for avoiding direct communication have been used, the most common being insufficient time. Indeed, effective cross-cultural intervention may take more than the regularly allotted brief interaction. Another form of resistance is the focus on activity, that is, a task orientation, which is sometimes used to control or mask anxiety in uncomfortable or unfamiliar situations (Devereux, 1967). Similarly, negating or repressing affective content due to the belief that expression of feelings is nonprofessional may help to defuse anxiety, but it avoids direct communication.

The provision of acceptable and appropriate health care in situations that involve diversity requires communication and psychosocial skills, as well as flexibility. Some providers feel that they are unduly taxed if asked to incorporate attitudes or behaviors that they associate with counselors, social workers, or mental health professionals. Our health care systems are not known for their flexibility or adaptability; indeed they usually represent values of efficiency and routinization. Furthermore most of us were educated to deal with individuals and not to think in terms of populations or subpopulations. Some health care workers believe that issues that involve groups or aggregates of people are irrelevant to their practices, which focus on individuals or small groups rather than cultural patterns or social issues or larger populations.

Resistance to issues related to racism, sexism, ageism, and similar issues is common. One cannot deny the need to deal with those issues, however, without ignoring a substantial part of social process and current events. When one orientation or set of values drives the provider's experiences and behavioral responses and another the consumer's, the provider still has an obligation to use his or her skills to recognize the issues and to foster the highest possible level of wellness. We live in a complex, multicultural society; exemption by occupational role from culturally congruent care for diverse peoples is unrealistic and inadequate, perhaps to the extent of being an ethical issue (Cortese, 1990).

Dependence on stereotypes also reinforces resistance to genuine interest and involvement. For instance, stereotypic associations with danger, violence, poor neighborhoods, limited ability, irresponsibility, or "noncompliance" tend to discourage relativistic approaches and communicative efforts.

On the other hand, sensitivity with inadequate knowledge can result in fear of mismanaging situations and lead to resistance, as when anxiety over "hurting feelings" leads to avoidance of communication and opposition to adapting standard interventions to meet nonconventional needs. Perhaps the most common fear is that what one says will be misunderstood or taken out of context or that what is tried will be rejected. Willingness and ability to accept, affirm, and manage diversity in health care settings depends upon confidence gained through knowledge and practice of applicable skills.

Providers are often unfamiliar with appropriate intervention and communication strategies in situations that involve persons or groups dissimilar from themselves or that involve circumstances beyond their own experience. Discomfort based on unfamiliarity and threatened personal integrity encourages resistance and defensiveness. The status quo is familiar and may be more acceptable than change (or the risk implied in behaviors aimed at change), particularly to those with little experience with minority statuses. Change may also be associated with a risk of power, that is, with the relinquishment or redistribution of power. Fear of loss of whatever control one has can be very threatening. The idea that one's present approach may be somehow insufficient is threatening when a significant investment has been made in a recognized, respected, and demanding status and role. Nonetheless, lack of interest in diversity as a factor in care provision is unrealistic. Health care providers generally want to provide quality care. Given the frequency with which they face situations involving diversity in the United States today, they cannot afford to be unprepared to manage them effectively.

Communication Skills

The goals of diversity-affirming communication skills are the facilitation of mutual understanding and the prevention of unanalyzed and inappropriate cultural or subcultural imposition (Pedersen et al., 1981). Accomplishment of those goals expedites the provision of appropriate and acceptable, that is, culturally congruent health care (Leininger, 1985b, 1988b).

Articulating the Problem from
the Client's Point of View

In clinical settings it is often impossible to avoid making judgments that attach positive or negative values to behaviors. Understanding of specific, concrete situations helps to relieve frustration, increase response options, and increase competence and confidence in managing diversity. Assessment and decision making are facilitated by the ability to understand the client's (emic) perspective.

The first cross-cultural communication skill area emphasizes articulation of the problem from the client's point of view. There are several specific behaviors that have been adapted from Pedersen (1988) and tested by the authors to facilitate that clarification process:

1. Explicate and define, as accurately as possible, the thinking and feelings of all involved as they relate to the client's presenting problem.
2. Reflect those feelings in noncritical verbal descriptions of the emotions contained in or expressed by the client's behavior.
3. Briefly review and summarize with the client (and others, as indicated) what he, she, or they have observed over a period of time.
4. Avoid unnecessary abstract or unfamiliar terms.
5. Restate what the client reveals in less vague and more specific ways.
6. Use the same time perspective that the client uses, whether past, present, or future.
7. Keep communications to the client congruent; avoid giving mixed or conflicting messages.
8. Indicate appreciation and respect for the dignity of the individual, the client's group, and his, her, or their situation. (Negative statements or "put-downs" denote an absence of respect.)

To assist with conceptualization of the problem from the client's point of view, articulation triangles (Figure 2.1) (adapted from Pedersen et al., 1981) are useful to define relationships among the client, the provider, and the problem.

The client has a relationship with the problem as he, she, or they see it. Initially, the influence of the health care provider is less than that of the problem (Figure 2.2). To help develop the ability to see both the insider (emic) and outsider (etic) perspectives, that is, to see both the client's and the health care provider's points of view, consider the following:

1. Who is the client?
2. What does the client view as the problem?
3. What does the problem mean to the client?
4. From the client's perspective, who has control over the problem?

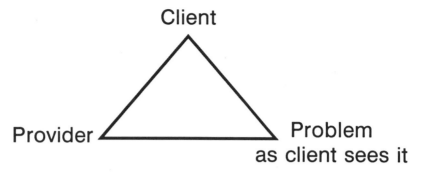

Figure 2.1. Basic Articulation Triangle

5. What are the potential consequences if the health care provider imposes his or her point of view? For example, might the client become resistant ("noncompliant")?
6. How are chances for effective communication and intervention increased or decreased by understanding the problem from the client's perspective?

A Practice Scenario

Tasha is an obese 13-year-old female. She attends a small school, where she is socially marginal because of her appearance and poor hygiene. Tasha lives with her mother, Samantha Adams, an attractive, 35-year-old, divorced, professional woman who is embarrassed by her daughter's appearance. Samantha attributes "Tasha's problem" to others as the result of an (undocumented) "glandular imbalance that will go away as she matures," and to Tasha as the result of "sheer laziness." She rejects Tasha's apparent disinterest in her physical status and makes it clear that she thinks the expected norm for 13-year-old girls is an "obsession with, not neglect of " their appearance.

Also in the home is an 8-year-old brother/son, Tom, for whom Tasha is caretaker before and after school when their mother is at work. Tom uses Tasha's appearance against her when he can. He has learned that he can get away with teasing her when his friends are around, and that she will anger and retaliate when they are alone.

Tasha's teacher, Susan Blair, who is also significantly overweight, pays little attention to Tasha, who meets minimum standards in her schoolwork and is not disruptive in class.

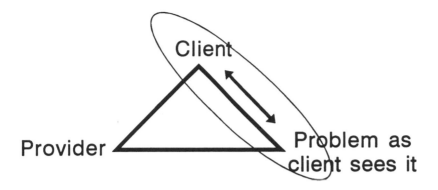

Figure 2.2. The client has a relationship with the problem as he, she, or they see it.

You are a health care professional recently assigned as a consultant for health care in Tasha's school. You notice her when doing seventh-grade health assessments because of her discomfort while disrobing for a scoliosis exam and the difficulty that her obesity posed when an accurate assessment was attempted. Also, while discussing nutrition with the third grade, you note a comment that Tom made about living with a "pig of a sister who eats everything in the house."

What do you think might be going on? Examine, using the articulation triangles in Figures 2.3 to 2.6, how the problem is likely to be viewed by each participant: Tasha (Figure 2.3), her mother Samantha (Figure 2.4), her brother Tom (Figure 2.5), and her teacher Susan (Figure 2.6). Do not assume that Tasha's weight is always the identified problem.

Discuss what might be needed in each case to result in shifts away from coalitions between each potential client perspective and the problem and toward one or more coalitions as you, the health care provider, communicate that you understand and accept alternative perspectives of the problem. For maximum effectiveness, the health care provider works with the client to handle the problem. Who is the client, and what will happen if you and the client form a coalition against the problem (Figure 2.7)? Try to assess the problem from the perspective of each individual involved.

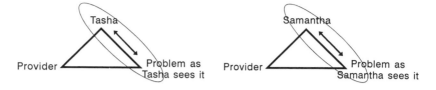

Figure 2.3. Tash's View for Scenario   **Figure 2.4.** Tasha's Mother's View

Figure 2.5. Tasha's Brother's View   **Figure 2.6.** Tasha's Teacher' View

Mutual Goal Formation

The formation of mutual goals will enable the client and health care provider to work together to resolve the problem. Discuss the development of mutual goals as illustrated in Figures 2.8 to 2.11. What are the pros and cons of alternative strategies to form the coalitions (illustrated in Figure 2.8, 2.9, 2.10, and 2.11) that would allow you

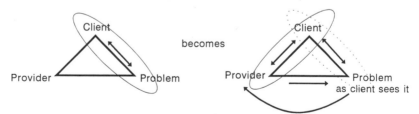

Note the changes in the relationship from client and problem to client and provider.

The provider and client now can work together toward problem resolution.

Figure 2.7. Formation of Coalition by Client and Provider Against Problem

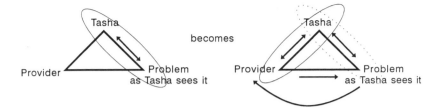

Figure 2.8.

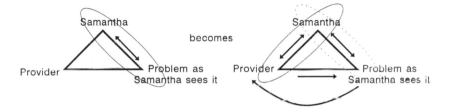

Figure 2.9.

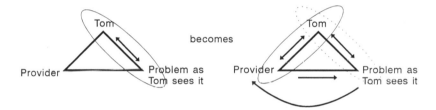

Figure 2.10.

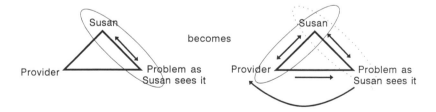

Figure 2.11. Client Provider Coalitions (Figures 2.8 to 2.11)

to help resolve the problem from the client's point of view? Keep in mind the value of personal integrity.

Recognizing and Managing Defensiveness

At times communication is associated with risk, such as when there is uncertainty about how exposure of reactions will be received, especially if the others have power or are in some way potentially threatening. When involved in a situation that is uneasy, defensiveness, anger, or hurt may occur.

Defensiveness connotes response to perception of threat and is usually accompanied by some rationalization or justification that maintains the status quo. Defensiveness occurs when personal security is perceived to be threatened. Whereas the nondefensive individual, whether client or provider, can focus on the client's needs, defensiveness leads to distraction as the need changes to having to defend the self. Providers, for example, may feel a need to defend their credentials or experience, while consumers might feel they must defend their ethnic origins, gender, past decisions, behavior patterns, status, or their adequacy in any of a large number of other ways.

To bring defensiveness to the surface so that it can be reduced, it is often helpful to state the obvious. For example, if it is noted that eye contact has been avoided, one might say, "Something was just said and most of you began to look around. What happened?" Stating the obvious in combination with an inference and a question might result in, "Something was just said that should have troubled or annoyed some people. Yet, everyone is acting as if it was not said. What's going on?" The implied may be stated, "Am I to assume that what was said was not heard or has no meaning to anyone?" or "I have the impression that there is too much discomfort with what was said to let your reaction show." There are countless ways to verbalize responses that focus on actual experiences.

There are several additional behavioral strategies that are useful for decreasing defensiveness (adapted from Pedersen, 1988):

1. Defensiveness may be revealed and identified through assessment of a client's expression, manner, or tone of response to understand, from the client's perspective, what the client's behavior means.
2. Humor, including that which is self-directed, is often valuable in diminishing defensiveness and building rapport.
3. Disclosing selected, culturally appropriate personal information can decrease defensiveness by promoting sharing and a sense of

acceptance. Interactions in scientific and biomedical settings tend to create barriers of impersonality between the provider and consumer. This becomes exaggerated when a client is expected to disclose personal information, often of an intimate nature, and a provider remains impassive to this one-sided situation.

4. Acknowledging and describing your own or the client's beliefs, behavior, or responses in nonjudgmental ways avoids defensiveness.

5. Eliciting information or help from others, including clients, minimizes defensiveness. Acknowledge your unfamiliarity with the client's culture; your interest is more likely to be valued than is pretending that you are familiar with it, or that cultural background is unimportant. Avoid the expectation that you are to know everything.

6. Being spontaneous without being reckless communicates regard for the situation and for the people involved. Exaggerated deliberation or stiltedness appears defensive and promotes defensiveness in clients.

7. Acknowledging defensiveness when it occurs gains respect for your honesty and integrity. There is no need to apologize for feelings. Analyze and acknowledge in specific terms what caused the defensive response.

8. Accepting responsibility for interactive or behavioral errors by openly acknowledging and apologizing for them reinforces realistic expectations for interaction.

9. Being flexible prevents frustrations. Plans are necessary for meeting goals, but flexibility is needed when it becomes apparent that the original plan is not congruent with the client's needs or expectations.

In dealing with defensiveness, the difficulty of acknowledging negative affect (for example, anger, disgust, distance, or disbelief) should be addressed. To be managed effectively, negative affect should be dealt with in terms that are as specific and as accurate as possible.

Recognizing and Reducing Resistance

The recognition, acknowledgment, and reduction of resistance as an interactive response is important in minimizing barriers to respectful and mutual communication between clients and providers. Resistance involves barriers to trust or opposition to the goal of mutual communication. Providers may find themselves resisting use of a client's perspectives in problem definition and resolution. Clients, on the other hand, may resist professional views of the problem, strategies, or goals.

Although it is a different phenomenon, resistance is similar to defensiveness as an interactive process. The increased probability of resistance and defensiveness occurring in situations that involve diversity reinforces the importance of understanding that what is done and said, verbally and nonverbally, has an impact.

The initial goal of managing resistance, like that of dealing with defensiveness, is its identification in specific rather than general terms (Pedersen, 1988). That often entails clarifying, specifying, or otherwise organizing information that is contained in ambiguous statements. Specific behavioral approaches facilitate recognizing and diminishing resistance (based on and adapted from Pedersen, 1988):

1. Demonstrate acceptance and understanding by clearly identifying the client's concern or understanding of the problem, whether or not it is addressed the same way by the client.
2. Carefully assess coping response patterns to stressful and other problematic situations. This includes one's own coping patterns. Such assessment promotes identification of patterns of resistant responses.
3. Ask questions, but alter them according to the client's cultural and linguistic expectations. For members of some groups only open questions are socially acceptable (for example, "How do you handle . . . ?"). For others, closed questions are preferred (such as, "Do you . . . ?"). Still others (including many traditional Native American groups) require indirect inquiries. Questions are cast in story-like scenarios to which the client may respond. For instance, "Some people find that when that happens it is best to . . ."
4. Recommended interventions are typically more acceptable to the client, and therefore less likely to meet with resistance, when explanations or instructions are adjusted to make them culturally appropriate. When working with members of Native American populations, for example, knowledge that the pattern of indirect suggestion indicated above is expectable (whether or not a specific individual responds to it) is valuable. It acknowledges sensitivity to the fact that clear directives have been associated historically with dishonor and dehumanizing loss of dignity and indicates

that the respectful provider considers the client capable of grasping the point and making an appropriate decision according to his, her, or their circumstances.

5. Open acknowledgment and confrontation of discrepancies between the views of the client and those of the health care provider can foster open, honest communication. Confrontation is not always to be avoided and is not used in angry or aggressive ways. Prediction, using knowledge about the client, of the probable interpretation and consequences of confrontation is important.

6. Accurately reflecting, clarifying, interpreting, and, perhaps, relabeling the client's behaviors, beliefs, or ideas can communicate both recognition and understanding of the client's perspective.

7. Develop awareness of and knowledge about the client's informal or natural support systems. The client is part of a larger system and seldom acts or makes decisions truly alone. For members of many groups, what health care providers view as an individual's problem is perceived as a symptom of a group-oriented rather than as an individual problem.

8. Reflect and adjust the voice, body position, and other aspects of communication to synchronize with those of the client.

Developing Recovery Skills

Affirming and managing diversity sometimes means venturing into unknown or potentially uncomfortable interactive situations. Often all goes smoothly, but mistakes occasionally occur. Since all behaviors, including those that are passive, communicate, mistakes are inevitable now and then. The goal is to be ready to manage them: to recognize, acknowledge, be nondefensive about, and intervene in them so as to facilitate mutual communication.

Recovery skills provide a repertoire of strategies to remedy mistakes (Pedersen, 1988). Recovery skills are needed when the provider has said or done something that aroused the client's anger or suspicion, otherwise distanced the client, finds that the client has become distant due to some other reason, or realizes that the resources available in that setting will not meet the client's needs.

Frequently, rapport can be recovered by verbally or nonverbally behaving in ways that reestablish confidence in the provider. Specific communication skills are relevant to interactive recovery, that is, getting out of trouble (Pedersen, 1988). For example:

1. Redirect attention from a controversial topic, or one that has created or reinforced barriers between the client and the provider, back to the basic problem.
2. Apologize for your gaffe or error. It is unreasonable for either you or the client to expect your communicative performance to be impeccable. Acknowledge your limitations (sometimes humor helps with this), while communicating your intent to learn how to avoid mistakes in the future.
3. Temporarily reverse the client and provider roles to solicit consultation from the client as a source of information for generating appropriate and acceptable solutions and alternatives. Recognize and acknowledge that your client knows more than you do about his or her culture or subculture.
4. Be able and willing to tolerate periods of silence.
5. Bring in an additional person or persons to mediate or act as "culture broker" (Weidman, 1973; Scott, 1981; Lefley, 1984) during a difficult exchange. This is critical when language or other cultural differences create barriers between the health care provider and the consumer.
6. Identify and develop metaphors or stories based on what the client has said as the foundations for explanations. Using words and analogies from the client's experience helps explanations fit his, her, or their perspective.
7. Identify an area of unmet need or opportunity that is not yet recognized by the client and build on it to the client's advantage.

Sometimes rapport with a provider cannot be recovered. The goal then is to try to ensure against loss of the client from the health care system in general and to encourage rapport with another provider. If conscientious assessment, effort, and evaluation of the relationship or situation indicates that it is not likely to be productive or rewarding for the client, carefully select an alternative, culturally appropriate, and acceptable provider and refer the client to that resource. Acting as a go-between to help the client negotiate access to the new provider may be important to retaining the client in health care (Pedersen, 1988). If premature termination becomes necessary, end the discussion or the relationship in a culturally appropriate way.

Development of recovery skills involves gaining confidence, which comes from successful practice and commitment to mutual communication as the most productive option. A lack of mistakes may suggest a failure to take risks, which in its passivity denies diversity and condones social distance. The authors take the stand that it is better to actively communicate than to try to avoid communication, since no action at all perpetuates social barriers and fails to acknowledge real and meaningful differences.

In sum, when assertive communication occurs, mistakes will also occasionally occur. No one communicates perfectly; "perfect" communication is not an appropriate goal. Even skilled communicators make mistakes, but they learn to correct and live with them. It is crucial to give oneself permission to take risks and to learn to recover when communicative problems arise.

Practice Strategies

The idea has been set forth that avoidance and ineffective management of difficult interactions cause troublesome feelings of loss of control and powerlessness, as well as compromise client outcomes. Such problems can be allayed with adequate knowledge and skills. Although practice is important to test and gain knowledge and skills, it is at times avoided because of the association of practice with interactive risk. Therefore it is important to practice in safe settings. To facilitate that, numerous practice strategies are provided to allow the opportunity to test knowledge and skills in settings that minimize risk. The strategies that follow are aimed at analysis of personal behaviors and characteristics in situations where awareness and sensitivity make discussion safe.

Starting with the Self

The processes involved in practice of skills related to diversity begin with the self. As a source of information, reflective interaction facilitates management of sensitive issues for the potential benefit of both provider and consumer (Damon, 1989).

Self examination is not always a risk-free and pleasant process, although acknowledging vulnerability in self introspection can encourage direct communication and bolster personal integrity. On the other hand, interacting with oneself does not incur the risks associated with exposure to others. The individual controls what is or is not disclosed, which minimizes need for defensiveness. Even if one decides not to expose the existence of a new or potentially different personal perspective, there is learning to be gained by observing oneself interact with both the self and others. Experience with diversity, however, depends on interaction with others.

The Role of Interaction and Discussion

Obtaining the material required for learning about diversity involves interacting with people, preferably with people from a variety of backgrounds. If individuals could obtain the exposure needed from people with whom they share obvious commonalities, there would be little need for in-depth exploration of differences.

Interaction and discussion of issues are efficient and effective ways to learn. Not all that is to be learned from others has to be discussed; however, validation of the meaning and impact of behaviors, thoughts, feelings, and values often requires verbalization. Oral comments encourage dialogue among people.

Discussion simulates face-to-face interactions among people whose backgrounds differ, although they each have personal assets based on their cultural backgrounds and past experiences. Their present values, knowledge, and skills can be called into play in a personal context. Because people talk about that which they know, real-life and day-to-day issues will automatically be included unless such sharing is hampered by discomfort, resistance, or decisions to "hold back."

Small Groups as Testing Sites

Small-group discussion is one way of testing interactive knowledge and skills. Small groups provide useful contexts in which to encourage participants to move beyond the comfort of assuming that the many rules that govern interactions with others are known and shared.

Cultural values and social expectations provide communicative rules to protect the self and others. Some providers may respond defensively to the suggestion of encountering diversity. The small-group context encourages acknowledgment of the possibility of dislike for or discomfort with the task at hand.

It is important to remember that values, thoughts, and feelings may not be communicated by overt behaviors. The realization that multiple individual experiences may appear the same, despite having different meanings and motivations, serves as a useful initiation point for discussion. Most adults have learned to match personal responses to specific contexts, for example, openly sharing, hiding, or disguising their responses. During interactions, people frequently react to voice tones and modulations, body language, innuendoes, and omissions but overtly respond only to the oral message. Sometimes oral messages are smoke screens. Whereas unfamiliar encounters may be awkward, small-group process can encourage replacement of automatic responses with responses that attend to meaning and context.

Discussion in groups of six to eight participants is a powerful strategy when the participants are able to trust others with meaningful information about themselves. In the small-group context, whether at school, at work, or in a clinical setting, involvement is not intended to be a commitment to public risk-taking or exposure of personal perspectives. Others may or may not think and feel similarly about the issues and topics involved in diversity, and exposure of personal experiences is never to be coerced. However, the opportunity for feedback and chance to try new reactions can be invaluable.

Interpersonal encounter requires living with the moments that work as well as with those that do not work. Although it is the presence of others and the uncertainty about how one is perceived that may make participants feel vulnerable, it is the absence of expecting perfection that most contributes to creating a safe environment for discussion.

The presence of a diverse audience changes the rules for interaction and thus enhances the possibility of continuing to gain understanding of different perspectives. Ironically, the audience along with the consent to learn about diversity potentially will decrease the likelihood of tolerance of avoidance, of "pulling rank" or making power plays, and of resorting to patronization.

Use of summary statements or brief stories that indicate how others have responded can help to stimulate sharing. One might say, for example,

When someone has risked exposing a feeling that they weren't sure was going to be accepted, it is usually helpful to have that feeling acknowledged without criticism. Some people establish and maintain eye contact, though not with the intensity of a fixed gaze. Others nod or lean toward the person indicating that they are listening. Someone may verbalize or name the emotion. Sometimes someone does not understand what the emotional tone is about, but would like to understand it, so they ask. Someone else may ask for information about what the person is feeling.

Providing a supportive atmosphere, that is, acknowledging feelings, beliefs, or values, does not mean that there is validation that those are appropriate, understood, or accepted by members of the group. It simply eliminates judgments that cause defensiveness or embarrassment. It is important to validate both the right to respond and variations in responses.

Getting people involved in group activities is not always easy. For some, discussion in ethnically or gender-mixed groups is contrary to cultural norms, can be frightening, or may involve disparate expectations. Tannen's (1990) research indicates that regional, ethnic, socioeconomic class, age, and gender variations result in different uses of language and patterns of communication. For example, when men and women are together in classes or groups, men tend to use a greater percentage of the discussion time. Language usage in groups may also affect African Americans differently from European Americans. The oral tradition is an integral aspect in the lives of many African Americans (Whitten & Szwed, 1970; Anderson, 1986). Because of differences in language characteristics and usage, word meaning, intonations and styles of obtaining and giving information, many African Americans may feel intimidated in discussion groups. Individuals for whom English is a second language may also experience conversational difficulties.

It may be that some group members verbalize less than others. This does not mean that they do not contribute, or that the silent individuals have nothing to offer to the discussion. There are many ways to be attentive or inattentive, to give approval or disapproval, to recognize or ignore, and to encourage or discourage without the use of words. There is no need for defensiveness about silence. Silence is a powerful tool. In some cultures, silence has special meanings and uses.

Strategies and Activities for Practice

A number of activities are provided as examples for getting participants to use information about diversity that involves personal characteristics, such as beliefs, customs, values, feelings, and assumptions.

Role Plays for Practice

Role play provides a valuable technique for classroom and clinical practice of decision making and skills for use in situations that involve diversity. The following model is adapted from cross-cultural counselor Paul Pedersen's "Triad Model" (Pedersen et al., 1981; Pedersen, 1988) and has been successfully utilized in both classroom and clinical settings that involve health care delivery to diverse populations. This role play approach has proven to be a valuable tool for disclosing aspects and depths of interaction that otherwise often remain covert.

The technique is very simple. Place three chairs in the positions indicated in Figure 2.12. Be sure that all participants can see and hear each other. Assign "Provider," "Client," and "Challenger" (which is similar to the client's alter ego) roles to three participants. They assume positions in the chairs and are provided with a brief scenario, including a congruent setting (for example, family planning clinic, community focus group, etc.). Interaction is initiated between the Provider and the Client. As the Provider and the Client converse, the Challenger communicates (verbally and nonverbally) what the client cannot or does not express. The challenger might include resistant and defensive responses, beliefs, or practices that conflict with those the Provider describes, and phenomena such as lack of familiarity with the proposed course of action. In essence, the Challenger points out for the client obstacles to what the health care provider does or proposes.

Allow the exchange to continue at least three to five minutes. Then stop it to analyze the participants' roles and their responses to each others' role enactments. For example, how did the Provider feel when confronted by the things that the Challenger said or gestured and that the Client did not articulate (but presumably might have wanted to)? What prevented the Client from saying those things for himself or herself? How might the interaction have been altered to

Challenger   **Client**   **Health care provider**

Figure 2.12. Role-Play Model

maximize mutual understanding and openness and to minimize defensiveness and resistance by the Client and/or the Provider?

If the Provider role is perceived as potentially uncomfortable or threatening, consider adding a fourth role, "Backup," as illustrated in Figure 2.13. The Backup role provides quiet but audible support for the Provider, not taking over the provider's role, but, rather, supplying suggestions for direction of the conversation.

The role play is particularly effective when videotaped and replayed for group analysis and discussion of both verbal and nonverbal aspects of the interaction.

Other Activities

The following exercises include two major types of activities, options, and tasks. Since participants must start somewhere, tasks are sequenced without options. Tasks are activities in which all participants have experience. Although they involve the use of such personal resources as listening, writing, and making judgments, there is minimal exposure of personal information. For the most part, tasks involve interaction with oneself, but use of the tasks in group contexts facilitates learning about other's views.

Options allow participants to pick and choose activities. It is anticipated that participants may develop additional options for interaction content and issues related to diversity.

Figure 2.13. Expanded Role Play

Activity 1

TASK 1: The first task is to observe a 1- to 2-minute portion of a discussion between members of a dyad or among three to four people. Select a situation in which you are not expected to participate, and in which the people are not aware that they are being observed. To observe both verbal and nonverbal behavior, you need to be able to see their faces and bodies. (If you are unable to find the needed situation, observe a segment of a televised conversation.)

TASK 2: Write down the conversation and the nonverbal behaviors of each conversant.

TASK 3: Use the grid (Table 2.1) to analyze the interaction:

a. For each conversant check verbal and nonverbal behaviors that can be attributed to each category.

b. Note the behaviors that can be attributed to the similarities (S) or to the differences (D) among the conversants.

c. Identify the values that are indicated by the verbal and nonverbal behaviors.

TASK 4:

a. Replace one of the participants in the conversation with yourself. How would the verbal and nonverbal behaviors change?

b. Which of the categories listed above would differ if you replaced an original participant?

Table 2.1 Cultural Values Evident in Interactions

Category	Person 1	Person 2	Person 3	Person 4
Gender				
Ethnicity				
Age				
Job/Position[1]				
Role/Relationship[2]				
Education				
SES[3]				
Language				
Other (Identify)				

NOTES: S—Similarities among conversants
D—Differences among conversants
[1]For example, white or blue collar, minimum wage earner, laborer, professional.
[2]For example, relative, casual acquaintance, friend, spouse, parent, child.
[3]For example, socioeconomic status or class (poor, working class, middle class, upper class).

    c. How did your feelings differ when you were an active participant rather than a passive observer?

    d. Were your verbal and nonverbal behaviors congruent with your feelings?

    e. What did the other person(s) think of you?

    f. How did your presence impact on the other participants or the conversation?

TASK 5: Put the original person back in the scenario and join the conversation.

    a. How would the verbal and nonverbal behaviors change?

    b. Which of the listed categories (Table 2.1) were most influential in the interaction?

    c. What happened to your feelings? Did they change?

    d. How did your presence change the course of events during the interaction?

OPTION 1:

   a. In a small group, have a volunteer present a brief description of a scenario.

   b. Each participant is to categorize the values indicated in the scenario according to the grid in Table 2.1. Discuss what prompted your fit of the behaviors into specific categories.

   c. Note the similarities and differences among classifications and identification of values.

OPTION 2: Compare and contrast your responses and feelings for your two simulated participations (Tasks 4 & 5).

   a. How did others see you during the last two interactions?

   b. To what extent can you rely on the verbal and nonverbal behaviors of the other participants in the group to validate your perceptions of how you came across?

OPTION 3: Evaluate Activity 1 by answering the following:

   a. What have you learned about your influence on interactions?

   b. What have you confirmed about how others see you relative to how you see yourself?

Activity 2

Since conversation styles change in response to the context of others' styles, it is useful to note and discuss ways of interacting in different groupings.

TASK 1: Form groups of three to four people based on gender, age, specialty, ethnic background, education major, common interest, or conversation style (for example, placing the fast talkers or quiet people together).

TASK 2: Read the following case study, which involves sex and gender roles, and identify your own responses to it.

A Case Study Involving Sex Role and Gender

Pat, Dale, Max, and Leslie are nurses who often work the evening shift on the same unit. Leslie mentioned to Dale, the other male RN on the unit, that he was getting tired of being assigned "heavy" tasks such as subduing assaultive patients or moving weighty ones, while "Pattie and Maxine push wheel chairs and pass out food trays. I've had it with this," he told Dale. "It's time we really shared these tasks! Let's tell the girls we don't like this. It isn't fair."

Max and Pat listened to Leslie's "protest," agreeing that tasks could be more equitably distributed and that gender was not a valid reason for deciding who was to do what. Later in the evening, a patient was admitted to the unit. Dale asked him if he had had dinner, to which the patient responded that he had not. Dale mentioned it to Maxine and went to pass medications. Later, noticing that the new patient still did not have a tray, "Hey, Max," he said, "Mr. Jones still hasn't had supper. Are you going to get a tray together for him?"

Max looked surprised, "Me? Why me?" "But, Max," Dale interceded, "You or Pat always do that." Pat said, "I thought you and Dale wanted tasks shared. You are just as capable of pulling together a tray in the kitchen for your patient as Pat is or I am!" Leslie started with "But you girls . . ." as Maxine ducked into another room with a quick "You can drop the 'girls' stuff, Les, unless you and Dale are happy being 'boys.' "

Meanwhile, Pat joined Dr. Sanchez with a patient who had recently had surgery following an injury that involved his genitals. Dr. Sanchez waved her away with "Go get one of the men, please. This really is none of your business." "Excuse me, Dr. Sanchez," Pat responded, "It is my business. Mr. Purdue is my patient. I need to see what has been done and what needs to be done in order to care for him well. It really does not matter where his surgery has been. I cannot monitor change if I cannot see it now."

TASK 3: Each person is to use 1 to 3 minutes to orally identify his or her perceptions of the case study.

TASK 4: Discuss the case study, identifying the issues from male and female perspectives.

  a. What assumptions and stereotypes are apparent?
  b. Indicate the stereotypes and assumptions on the following grid (Table 2.2).
  c. Identify the stereotypes to which each character in the case study responded. What assumptions are associated with each stereotype? What patterns are apparent within gender subgroups?
  d. Identify the defensive behavior of each nurse.

Table 2.2 Identifying Stereotypes and Assumptions

	Stereotypes	Assumptions
Pat		
Dale		
Max		
Leslie		

TASK 5:

a. Identify the implications of labels such as "the girls" or "the men?"

b. Identify the implications of gender stereotypes in female-dominated professions such as nursing.

c. Are the members of female-dominated professions empowered to control their professional destinies?

d. What happens to males who join female-dominated professions? Who has the power in such professions?

e. What objective evidence indicates the location of the power?

TASK 6: Discuss:

a. The purposes or goals that are met by maintaining distinctive sex and gender roles.

b. How life would differ if each participant's gender were changed.

c. The advantages of sex- and gender-role equity.

d. The disadvantages of sex- and gender-role equity.

TASK 7: Discuss what the group participants think about the positions taken by each of the four nurses.

OPTION 1: Write down the name of each person in the group (use Table 2.3).

a. Identify and enter beside your name how you usually contribute to discussions and how you contributed to the discussion of the above case. Use the grid below to help organize your observations.

b. Identify, to the extent possible, how the other participants in the group usually contribute to discussion and how they contributed to this discussion. Use the grid (Table 2.3) to help organize your observations.

c. Have a designated person write on a surface that everyone can see (such as a chalkboard, flip chart, or transparency), the major interaction behaviors that have been identified by each group member.

Table 2.3 Interaction Behaviors Response Grid

*How was the group composed (by gender, age, a characteristic [please name], etc.)?*_____

Names	Usual Interaction Behavior	Present Interaction Behavior	Agree	Disagree

NOTE: Interaction behaviors may include offering information; clarifying; encouraging, e.g., nodding, responding "ah-huh"; challenging comments; attacking issues; confronting; debating; playing the "devil's advocate"; adding personal anecdotes; speaking without getting recognition from the leader; raising a hand for recognition; withdrawal after a substantial contribution, or numerous other interactive possibilities.

    d. Compare your responses on the grid with those on the board. Indicate your own agreement or disagreement with the patterns indicated on the board.

OPTION 2: Discuss how the group managed the above tasks.

    a. Was there an expectation that everyone contribute to the discussion? How was that communicated?

    b. What roles were taken by the group members? For example, did someone assume a leadership role or a peacemaker role?

Activity 3

Have someone in the group describe an example of an interaction with a client that involved ethnicity.

TASK 1: In a small group:

    a. Make two (2) columns on a chalkboard or flip chart. Identify the client's perceptions of the problem in one column. Then, based on the health care providers' perceptions, list the problems in the second column.

b. Identify the source(s) of the problems, for example, medical, familial, cultural, gender, physical, social, psychological, religious, etc.
c. Have each group member individually rank order the three most important problems that will require intervention or services.
d. Share the results of the individually rank-ordered priorities.

TASK 2: After rank ordering the problems that require intervention, discuss what the rank order implies about whose perceptions and values are most important.

a. Which of the client's values are evident in his or her list?
b. What provider values are evident from the listing of problems?
c. How do the provider's values compare to those of the client?
d. Identify what information would be needed about the client in order to provide culture-specific care. For example, what is included in the maintenance of his or her ethnic identity?
e. Discuss how you would obtain the needed information.
f. In interacting with the client, about what do you need to be concerned? For example, are there rituals related to ethnicity, gender, religion, or other characteristics?
g. Assume that you will do or say something that may offend the client. How might the situation be effectively managed?

Activity 4

The following collage (Collage A: Where is Equality for Fred Nightingale?) may be used alone or in combination with the case study involving Pat, Dale, Max, and Leslie as a continuation of examination of sex-role and gender issues. The activity involves a combined individual-group approach.

TASK 1: As a group:

a. Identify and record the issues and topics contained in the collage.
b. On what stereotypes and myths are the issues/topics based?

OPTION 1: Use the chart in Table 2.4 to identify each individual's reasons for considering or not considering nursing as a career choice. If you are a nurse, change the item focus and indicate reasons for staying in nursing. Then, list those reasons to leave nursing.

Table 2.4 Gender Assumptions

	Reasons	Assumptions
Would Consider Nursing		
Would Not Consider Nursing		

NOTE: S—Based on Societal Expectations
C—Based on Cultural Belief or Myth

    a. For each item reason, list the related assumption(s). If unable to think of assumptions, go onto your next reason.

    b. Code the items "S" to represent normative, societal, behavioral expectation and "C" to represent cultural belief or myth.

OPTION 2: As a group, use a board or flip chart to make two lists, one marked "MALE" and the other "FEMALE." In each column, list the reasons that the male and the female group participants give for considering or not considering nursing as a career. (Omit the appropriate column if the group is homogeneous.)

    a. Discuss the values that are inherent in the reasons given by members of each sex.

    b. Identify and discuss the assumption(s) or issue(s) related to gender and sex.

    c. Identify and discuss the assumptions or myths that would be offensive to a male nurse and to a female nurse.

    d. What impact might repeated exposure to the noted assumptions have on a nurse?

Collage A: Where Is Equality for Fred Nightingale?

e. If the group is interdisciplinary and includes some nurses, discuss how the generated list of reasons differs between nurses and non-nurses.

Summary

Part II of *Promoting Cultural Diversity: Strategies for Health Care Professionals* provided a variety of approaches for care and communication in health care settings that involve diversity and for practice of relevant skills. To aid in development and understanding of a multicultural perspective, intervention modes involving cultural preservation, negotiation, and repatterning were presented, discussed, and illustrated.

The communication skills emphasize articulation of problems from clients' perspectives, recognition and reduction of resistance and defensiveness, and recovery skills. The cultural communication skill areas promote analysis of affective dimensions of relationships and mutual communication between providers and consumers. Avoidance of communication is presented as an inadequate option and perfect communication as an unrealistic goal. Consequently, a repertoire of recovery skills are provided in preparation for managing impaired interactions.

In combination, the intervention and communication frameworks are useful in reducing social distance and maximizing potential for effective and acceptable care. However, it is practice that assures increased competence and confidence of skill areas. A selection of activities involving case studies and an issue-oriented collage is presented to assist with analysis.

Questions for Discussion

1. In what ways do differences between providers and clients, and, in particular, their expectations for communication and intervention, impact on provision of care?
2. How could health care providers be better prepared to work with multicultural populations?
3. What communication skills are particularly relevant to situations involving diversity?

4. How might decreasing provider defensiveness affect provision of health care?
5. What conditions of cross-cultural contact might lead to increased interactive harmony?
6. What conditions of cross-cultural contact might lead to increased hostility?
7. What are some barriers to accurate and open communication across cultures?
8. In what type of circumstances might cultural repatterning or restructuring be an appropriate approach to intervention?
9. How would you differentiate culturally trained health care providers from other providers?
10. How can health care best deal with the issue of time, which often limits opportunities for communication and development of appropriate intervention goals?
11. What incentive(s) do health care providers have to consider cultural and subcultural variables in their work with clients?
12. How can the flexibility required to provide appropriate and culturally congruent care be reconciled with the inflexibility that characterizes many aspects of health care systems?

Myths for Discussion

1. It is a myth that minority or subordinate issues can be handled appropriately only by those trained to recognize them and/or by those with other vested interests (such as being a member of a minority group).
2. It is a myth that sensitivity, awareness, knowledge, and skills do not work with low-income and other minority clients because members of those populations tend to be poor verbalizers, unwilling to defer gratification, uncooperative, insistent on immediate symptom resolution, and resistant to change (Lorion & Parron, 1985).
3. It is a myth that altering care or treatment procedures to accommodate cultural variables is unnecessary because any intelligent person, or even one with some basic common sense, can adjust.
4. It is a myth that treating people differently because of racial, religious, ethnic, cultural, gender, or other characteristics implies prejudice and discrimination.

5. It is a myth that it is not worthwhile to focus on one's own cultural values and social norms, since only the clients' matter.

Notes on the Myths

1. It is a myth that minority or subordinate issues can be handled appropriately only by those trained to recognize them and/or by those with other vested interests (such as being a member of a minority group).

There are several arguments against limiting training for diversity to those who are overtly involved with minority group status. The most compelling reason is that noninvolvement by members of majority groups condones and perpetuates social inequity. For example, abandoning concern for health care of ethnic minority individuals to those health care providers who are also members of ethnic minority groups would leave minority consumers underserved. Members of ethnic minority groups are underrepresented in most professional categories. For example, 12% of the United States' population is African-American, but only 4% of the nation's registered nurses are black (American Nurses' Association, 1987). The result may be overburdened minority professionals and underserved minority consumers, which in both cases perpetuates inequitable access to resources. There are simply not enough minority health care providers to meet minority consumers' needs, so whether or not interethnic situations are considered preferable, they are necessary. Denial of that statistical reality is more likely to represent avoidance of specific subgroups' needs than concern for their care.

It cannot be assumed that clients always need or want providers with social characteristics similar to their own. Sometimes they do not. For example, consumers may believe that those providers least like themselves are the most expert, or that they are unlikely to threaten anonymity with reports to mutual acquaintances. Occasionally clients indicate a preference for providers of specific backgrounds, but more commonly acceptance of providers is based on competence and attitude. Any provider who affirms diversity and is culturally sensitive, aware, knowledgeable, and skillful is typically able to intervene effectively on behalf of most clients.

Another reason to promote training for cross-cultural health care is that there are inside and outside perspectives to every situation and advantages to each. The insider is immersed in the situation, knows it intimately, and understands what it is like to experience a given set of circumstances. Due to closeness to the situation, the insider also has difficulty being objective about it. The outsider lacks the insider's intimate and subjective knowledge of the situation and must struggle to understand what that experience is likely to be like. However, the outsider may have the advantage of objectivity, which is lost to the insider, and may be able to provide alternatives of which the insider is unaware.

2. *It is a myth that sensitivity, awareness, knowledge, and skills do not work with low-income and other minority clients because members of those populations tend to be poor verbalizers, unwilling to defer gratification, uncooperative, insistent on immediate symptom resolution, and resistant to change (Lorion & Parron, 1985).*

The intervention modes and communication skills presented in this book are not limited in application. They function as tools for decreasing or avoiding barriers by empowering health care providers. There is evidence that providers who feel confident with their clients are more likely to have positive attitudes toward them (Fine, 1982). On the other hand, negative stereotyping of clients as resistant risks imposition of a self-fulfilling prophecy that leaves the client unserved and the provider impotent. The tendency to prefer certain types of clients (typically the "YAVIS," or those that are young, attractive, verbal, intelligent, and potentially successful) and to avoid others (for example, the "QUOIDS," that is, those that appear quiet, unattractive, old, indigent, and stupid) should be recognized by all providers, as should the relationships between those tendencies and powerlessness (Pedersen, 1979, 1981). If real barriers between specific providers and clients are detected and understood in specific terms, utilization of recovery skills can help ensure that the clients are not lost to health care systems. In some cases clients are best transferred to the care of someone else. In most cases, however, significant differences can be successfully bridged.

Educated Americans tend to use many abstract concepts and terms and to be quite verbal. Professional jargon often complicates communication for those socialized to different cultural or subcultural groups. In contrast, persons with relatively traditional orientations tend to use simple and concrete terminology. They may also be more oriented toward the present, perhaps even the survival-level present, than is the typical middle-class professional who is accustomed to long-term investments (such as advanced education) and their long-term rewards. Resistance to professional advice may be the result of limited information or misconception about probable outcomes, conflicting beliefs and/or practices, past experience that suggests caution or suspicion, or simple fear of the unknown.

There are many ways of knowing; science is not the only one. The client who does not have vast knowledge of or experience with allopathic medicine is not working in a void. Rather, he or she usually has at least a working knowledge of folk and/or popular (that is, over the counter) medicine, or even extensive knowledge of alternative systems of care (for example, the hot-cold theory that is prevalent among Hispanic and some Asian populations, aruvedic medicine among groups from the Indian subcontinent, or various other systems of understanding and managing health and illness [Foster & Anderson, 1978]).

To the uninitiated (and to some of the initiated), the systems of treatment and care that predominate in the United States risk dehumanization and loss of personal integrity because they reflect the following assumptions:

a. That "normal" is a shared idea. Actually, "normal" is a statistical phenomenon and represents what is expectable and happens most often, given a specified set of conditions. What is different or deviates from the norm then becomes "abnormal." That which members of groups consider normal is patterned by culture, class, and time. Consider what the norms were for health and illness a century ago, or what they might be in the future. Is it normal to be worried about plague or smallpox in the United States today? Were you concerned about your cholesterol level a decade ago?

b. That individuals are the basis of society. America is probably the most highly individuated society in the world. Most societies are far more oriented toward groups. One Asian student described this succinctly by noting that in her culture she is a small "i" and her family is the large "I." She felt uncomfortable putting herself first, even as symbolized by capitalization of a pronoun. It is common in our society to risk alienation and to highly value personal freedom and independence. Those are culture-specific patterns. Indeed, for peoples of many societies the signs of illness experienced by a group member are interpreted as a problem with the group, not within the individual.

c. That problems fit into academic or other culturally prescribed, artificial categories. In many societies health problems are not conceptualized as separate from other misfortunes, and physical illness as not separate from generalized illness or mental illness. Nor is health care always viewed as isolated from religious or other spiritual types of healing.

d.   That only one system of medicine will be used. In many parts of the world, the first thing that health care workers do, to minimize untoward interactions, is inquire into other treatments being used concurrently with biomedicine. Access to various folk systems is available in the United States, particularly in urban areas, and they are utilized for their familiarity, personal attitudes, low costs, accessibility and availability, compatibility of explanatory models, and lack of intrusive testing.

e.   That the client must fit the system, rather than the system adapt to the client. Culturally congruent care and effective communication and intervention require consideration of the client's perspective and understanding.

3. It is a myth that altering care or treatment procedures to accommodate cultural variables is unnecessary because any intelligent person, or even one with some basic common sense, can adjust.

Common sense is valuable, but it goes only so far and is based upon insights gleaned from the past in specific cultural contexts and settings. Furthermore, it is often expected that the client should do the adapting, which hinders successful intervention in many situations. A balanced combination of sensitivity, awareness, knowledge, and skills provide tools for expansion and adaptation to any situation. As one student put it, "Don't leave home without them!"

4. It is a myth that treating people differently because of racial, religious, ethnic, cultural, gender, or other characteristics implies prejudice and discrimination.

This is a frequently heard excuse to avoid dealing with issues that are part of social process. The problem with "color blindness" and other aspects of NOT acknowledging diversity and treating people differently (according to that diversity) is that it denies variations in their real-life experiences. Advocacy of a "color-blind" society, for example, functions to condone and maintain institutionalized racism within that society by denying that built-in barriers to equal opportunity to access status, power, and wealth have impact on peoples' lives. This approach also fails to attempt or allow change of those social facts.

This myth is part of an ideology that serves to justify an inequitable status quo. It may be simpler to ignore differences than it is to deal with them, but ignoring them supports continuation of unequal opportunity.

5. It is a myth that it is not worthwhile to focus on one's own cultural values and social norms, since only the clients' matter.

Providers and consumers interact. Their cultural baggage interacts with them. A major component in understanding others is first realizing from where you are coming. Clarifying your values and how they were acquired is crucial to having an accepting attitude toward those of others. To minimize the intrusion of unacknowledged biases when attempting to understand and appreciate someone else, cross-culturally competent health care personnel learn to know themselves well.

Most of what we know about getting along in society we learned through socialization processes that go unnoticed and are taken for granted. It takes a continuously critical and astute observer to approximate the kind of relationship that we have with ourselves.

Part III   Application: Case Studies and Collages

Introduction

It is recommended that practice scenarios be used as exercises to test analytical skills and to stimulate discussions. Numerous situations are presented here and others are available. For example, Brislin et al., (1986) provide a collection of intercultural interactions for analysis. With an emphasis on health care, Galanti (1991) supplies a compilation of case studies from American hospitals.

Part III of *Promoting Cultural Diversity: Strategies for Health Care Professionals* introduces a selection of case studies and collages with which to practice the analytical and communication skills presented in Parts I and II. Strategies for organizing the practice sessions and utilizing the case studies and collages were suggested in Part II.

The case studies function as exercises that involve common areas of cultural diversity and/or inequity. The scenarios reflect real life and are complex. Many of the case situations, despite their identified emphases, actually involve multiple areas of concern. The thematic areas of the cases include sex role and gender, disparity in socioeconomic status, ethnicity, age, health conditions, and race. Although based on actual experiences, all names used in the case studies are fictitious and details have been adapted for anonymous presentation in the exercises.

In the final case study, a detailed analytical model is presented. A case involving race was selected to exemplify analysis because institutionalized racism is a phenomenon that many health care providers find particularly difficult to recognize, analyze, and manage effectively. Although the case is presented in detail and reflects what actually transpired, other analytical approaches may also be appropriate.

It is important to remember that there is frequently not a single, correct analysis of a situation. The case studies can be assessed, planned for, intervened in, and evaluated from a variety of perspectives. To stimulate consideration of multiple problem definitions and analytical approaches, a series of collages is also presented. The collages are composed of clippings from the popular press and emphasize a variety of themes.

Case 1: A Practice Situation Involving Social and Economic Differences

Beverly Larkin, the wife of one of the two patients in 7A, complained about the "large crowd" of people and their smoking in her husband's room. She questioned why one patient had so many "smelly and loud visitors," adding with contempt, "What kind of place is this anyhow?" Upon investigation, it was found that nearly a dozen people had come to see Percy Washington. Percy's visitors had collected the chairs in the room and from the hall and arranged them around Percy's bed. Two visitors sat on the bed and several more leaned against the wall and closet.

Percy, at times homeless but recently staying with his sister, Sadie Benson, had numerous friends from the street and shelters where he "hung out." The small hospital had a policy of accepting only occasional "charity cases," but Sadie had seen that Percy's medical assistance card was updated and renewed, now that he was using her address. Percy had not resisted efforts to get him cleaned up when he was first admitted, although he was less compliant about other regulations, such as those against having food and drinks brought onto the unit or smoking in his bed or room.

Marv Larkin, the patient in the other bed in Percy's room, made it clear that he felt imposed upon when his own visitor had no place to sit. Another chair was produced from behind the nurses' station. A nurse asked some of Percy's visitors to wait elsewhere until they could see Percy in turn. Marv made a gesture of disgust toward the others in the room, and, with a nod toward them, admonished his wife to watch her belongings so that "nothing disappears." Beverly gripped her handbag and, looking anxious, almost tearfully demanded a room change for her husband.

Eventually visiting hours were over, Percy was asleep and snoring, and the medical resident came by to check on how Marv was doing. Marv had the following to say to him:

> Look, I know you folks have to take these people in. They get sick like everyone else. But I work. I pay taxes. I even vote and give to the United Way and the volunteer fire department, for Pete's sake. I should not have to be exposed to this riffraff in the hospital—in my own room in the hospital! I am a sick man, you know. And my wife, she worries. She worries about everything. She worries about what might happen to me here with the likes of these people around. We have rights too, you know. How do you think I feel when I get flowers and he doesn't? How the hell do you think I would feel if MY friends came in here and saw him or those other people?

Questions for Consideration and Discussion

1. How would you respond to Marv Larkin?
2. What assumptions and stereotypes are being made about Percy Washington and his associates, and why are those assumptions and stereotypes dangerous?
3. What assumptions is Marv Larkin making about the medical resident?
4. What aspects of society allow Marv Larkin to feel adequately secure about the assumptions he is making to express them to the resident?
5. What responsibilities do health care providers have regarding patient advocacy in situations such as this?
6. What is the problem from the clients' points of view?
7. How is defensiveness apparent? How might it be diminished?
8. How is resistance evident? How might it be diminished?
9. As you envision a variety of ways of managing this situation, what recovery skills might be indicated?

Case 2: A Practice Situation Involving a Health Condition[1]

Emily is a 35-year-old mother of two small children. She is blonde and attractive, vivacious, and bright. She has a college degree in journalism and is working on a second one in a social science. She communicates (in writing because she cannot speak due to a physical impairment) that her greatest need is to be allowed "to contribute." Emily is a student in a health-oriented, open-enrollment elective course.

In her advisor's office, Emily tells her story, half on paper and half in gestures. Curious passersby poke their heads in; they hear the faculty member speaking but do not hear the replies. The listener begins to get a hint of what Emily's life might be like. He wonders what it would be like to marry and raise children without being able to talk.

Emily was a teenager when she required surgery for a tumor that left her voiceless. There were numerous and fairly severe neurological fine motor impairments as well, although those usually were not noticeable from a distance and her gross coordination is intact. Emily's writing is labored to the extent that the campus program for handicapped students provided a notetaker for her in class. Fortunately, Emily has become proficient on the word processor and had no trouble getting her papers and tests completed. Her work is imaginative and her viewpoint refreshing.

For about 2 years, Emily worked for a newspaper. She liked the job very much, but was laid off. She had never found another place that would hire her. Managers responded positively to her at first, but when they realized her handicap, advised her that they were "afraid that the available position would be too much" for her. It had been pointed out many times to Emily, by well-meaning people in both formal and informal circumstances, that there was really no reason for her to work. She could "play at going to school" if she liked; she has two healthy children who need her and a husband who can support her. "People imply that I should be grateful to have a husband! Why shouldn't I have a husband?" She also qualifies for disability support. She had been asked repeatedly why she should want to make such an effort to subject herself to the possibility of public humiliation with a job.

Emily reiterated that she had a single, tremendous need. "I can contribute," she insisted, "I want the opportunity to contribute like other people do. I do not need to be taken care of. I want to study the relationship between disabled people and society. But everybody tells me to go home and take it easy. Why doesn't society give me a chance?"

Questions for Consideration and Discussion

1. What is the problem from Emily's point of view?
2. How is defensiveness evident? How might it be diminished?
3. How is resistance evident? How might it be diminished?
4. As you visualize a variety of ways of managing this situation, what recovery skills might be indicated?
5. What possibilities exist for support in Emily's situation. How do they involve health care?
6. How is self-fulfilling prophecy related to this case study?

Case 3: Practice Situation Involving Race

Maynard Grayce is an African-American physician working on a private medical floor. With a European-American medical student, Maynard entered a patient's room and introduced himself. After a few minutes, both men left the patient. Later Maynard returned to the patient to check his dressing. Referring to the medical student, the man asked Maynard to "go get the real doctor so that he can order my pills."

Questions for Consideration and Discussion

1. What assumptions are being made by the patient in this situation?
2. How would you feel, or have you felt, in a similar situation?
3. How could Maynard Grayce or a third party effectively manage this situation with minimal risk to the provider-patient relationship and to personal integrity?
4. What recovery skills might be employed to salvage this exchange?
5. What is ethnicity and how does it differ from race?

Case 4: A Practice Situation Involving Ethnicity

An elderly Vietnamese man was admitted in congestive heart failure. Several family members were at his bedside day and night. One grown daughter of about 35 years of age was very demanding and in constant conflict with the staff. She made one request after another, frequently wanted the doctor called, and wanted a nurse always present in her father's room. Her requests were actually demands and there was considerable anger as well as anxiety facial expression.

The nurses reported making every possible effort to meet the needs of the patient and to satisfy the daughter, but to no avail. Increasingly defensive, a member of the staff reminded the daughter that her father was not the only patient on the unit. They also began to enforce visitors' hours and went out of their way to avoid the daughter.

Finally the staff decided to have a meeting to discuss the family's needs, to verbalize their feelings, to set limits to prevent manipulation of the staff, and to promote respect for the staff. At the meeting it became clear that there were mixed feelings among the staff. These varied from excusing the Vietnamese woman's behavior because of her presumed lack of familiarity with American hospital etiquette and protocol, to deep resentment that "those foreigners are telling us how to do our jobs!" The unit personnel decided that they needed to be consistent and to work with the family to resolve conflicts. The head nurse met with the family to inform them of the care that was being given and to explore their feelings. The behavior on the part of the family did not change. Mady Feinstein, a health care provider with cross-cultural training was asked to consult with the staff and family.

Mady knew that cultural transition for East Asian immigrant families can be very difficult (Sue, 1981; Shon & Ja, 1982; Lappin & Scott, 1982). Language, customs, beliefs, family organization, and family process within the context of a specific culture (in this case, Vietnamese of Chinese ethnicity) have impact on the situation. She met and talked with the patient's family, learning that the unmarried daughters were very concerned about their father's health and that their single brother was now dead.

Mady explained to the unit staff about strong group ties and that women in Confucian philosophy and tradition are expected to follow their fathers, spouses, or eldest sons. Having immigrated with only their widowed father, he is looked to for authority and leadership. The daughters have proscribed sets of paternal obligations, both spoken and unspoken, because it is parents who bring children into the world and care for them. They are more fluent in English than is their parent, so the eldest daughter feels it is her role to be his advocate and spokesperson.

Questions for Consideration and Discussion

1. How might this situation be handled effectively?
2. What is the problem from the client's (clients') point(s) of view?
3. How is defensiveness evident and how might it be managed in this case?
4. What does resistance mean in this scenario, and how might it be managed?
5. How might communication problems effectively be bridged?
6. What resources exist in your health care setting for providing culturally appropriate support to this family?
7. What have been your own experiences with migration, adjustment, and culture shock?
8. What have been your own experiences with immigrant individuals and families?
9. What roles can health care providers play in supporting this family?
10. What intercultural communication skills do you expect to be demonstrated by Mady?

Case 5: A Practice Situation Involving Age

Cheryl blew out the candles on the cake and imagined that people wished that they represented more years than they did. She thanked the rest of the team for the surprise celebration, but doubted whether the one more year to her credit would make much difference. She knew that she was as old as some of the other social workers, and older than some, but she knew that the "petite little girl look" that so many told her was a blessing actually cost her dearly in respect.

She felt that Dr. Campbell treated her like a 10-year-old. He asked her to get someone else if he wanted to discuss a complicated case and had once referred to her as a "Candy-striper." Worse yet, Dr. Patel thought she was too young to know about the kinds of situations that many cases involved. While adolescents tended to ignore her as a professional or saw her as "just another kid," older patients wrote her off as too inexperienced to be able to give them competent care and direction. Even her sister, less than a decade older than she, got irritated at being mistaken for Cheryl's mother. Cheryl knew she knew her stuff, but feared she would have to be "a hundred and eight" to have anyone take her or her competence seriously. She had so looked forward to getting out of school and not being treated like a student anymore! Then she found out that qualifications to practice did not ensure much status.

This evening Cheryl visited Mr. Mathewson on the cardiac rehabilitation unit. Mr. Mathewson had grandchildren Cheryl's age, and he was not about to listen to them either. He did not want to get up, or to exercise, or to eat the food that arrived on his tray, and most of all he had no intentions of thinking about where he would go or how he would manage when he was discharged. He told Cheryl that all he wanted was some "real food, none of this plastic stuff with all the goodness zapped out of it," and he didn't want to be cared for by someone who had to use a stool to reach the equipment hook-ups on the wall over his bed. Cheryl explained that she was not a nurse, but, rather, a social worker, and that she had come to discuss his discharge plans. Later Dr. Campbell came in to examine his patient and, on her way by the room, Cheryl heard him tell Mr. Mathewson that he would have someone find him "a real social worker with some mileage on her" to help make his discharge arrangements.

Questions for Consideration and Discussion

1. As Cheryl's colleague, how would you support her?
2. What impact might Cheryl's apparent youth have on the situation if she was a health care consumer rather than a provider?
3. What is the problem? Whose problem is it?
4. How might defensiveness affect the situation?
5. How might resistance affect the situation?
6. What assumptions might resistance to a youthful provider be based on?
7. What issues in addition to age may be involved in Cheryl's situation?

Case 6: A Practice Situation
Involving Sex Role and Gender[2]

Mark is a nurse. That simple fact is met at times with disbelief. Whatever the stereotypes may be of "nurses," they apparently do not readily include good looking, 6'3" males. Mark's introduction to the consequences of bias against men who are nurses occurred in high school when the names of seniors and the schools they would attend after graduation were listed in the school's front hall. Mark's name and the hospital diploma program that he had selected were not included on the list. Later in nursing school he had to fight for the same opportunities that were planned into the clinical experiences of his female classmates. Due to intervention by an advocate on the faculty, Mark was allowed obstetrical and gynecological experience comparable to that of his colleagues. The other man in the program with him was not afforded the same opportunity.

Several years later Mark completed an RN-to-BSN program and entered a masters degree program in critical care nursing. His initiation to graduate school began with a security guard who, encountering an unfamiliar male in a female-dominated domain, stopped him on his way into the nursing building and demanded to know his business there. Since Mark had not yet completed registration and acquired an identification card, he was allowed to enter only because he happened to have with him a piece of correspondence addressed to him from the school.

Mark's perception is that his nursing education prepared him well as a critical care nurse, but that it punished him for being male, or, as he puts it, "for not being female." He realizes that this is a simple reversal of an old societal theme, but it seriously impeded development of a positive attitude toward the school, the program, and feelings of acceptance and cohesion. Some aspects of his experience were relatively minor. Restroom privacy, for example, was compromised by having to share a "unisex" facility in which use of the urinal, which was open to the room, would have risked exposure to anyone who entered. More bothersome was the attitude that he was at times considered overly aggressive by faculty, despite their advocacy of assertiveness for contemporary nurses. Even at work on the intensive care unit, Mark often feels that he can not win. When he assumes a leadership role in a clinical situation, his accomplishments are attributed to his gender rather than his skill and ability as a nurse. Although he typically feels penalized when assertive, when he does not assert himself he risks the negativity of those who "expect more" of nurses who are men.

Questions for Consideration and Discussion

1. What gender stereotypes are associated with nursing and how are they perpetuated?
2. What gender stereotypes are associated with medicine or other health care disciplines? How are those stereotypes perpetuated?
3. How do gender stereotypes affect opportunities in your organization?
4. Approximately 96% of nurses are female and 88% of physicians are male (Katzman & Roberts, 1988). Why are there not more men in nursing and more women in medicine?
5. How do prejudice and discrimination influence this situation?
6. How could fellow students and practitioners effectively support individuals in Mark's situation?
7. How could faculty and supervisors effectively support individuals in Mark's situation?
8. What can be done to alleviate sex role and gender bias?

Case 7: A Practice Situation
Involving Socioeconomic Differences

Katy is a young mother without an income. Having recently removed herself from an abusive marital situation, she filed for a divorce on Tuesday and applied for a job on Wednesday. She could have had the job, but when she figured out what it paid and what child care cost, it became clear to her that she "could not afford to work." She has become depressed, hypertensive, and is gaining weight at a rate that alarms her.

Katy went to a nearby health care clinic with some trepidation because she "really wasn't all that sick." There in the waiting room she read a magazine reprint of an old article by Maxine Kumin (1983) titled "It's Very Hard to Say I'm Poor." Katy concurred; it certainly is, she thought. When her name was called and she presented herself, she was asked what type of health insurance she had. Not knowing what to do, she murmured that she had none and left the clinic. The receptionist frowned at the incomplete form, tossed it in the wastebasket, and returned to her paperwork.

Questions for Consideration and Discussion

1. Where and how do individuals in Katy's situation qualify for health care?
2. What are the pros and cons of a health care industry in which access is a privilege rather than a right?
3. What are some of the long-term effects of limited health care for Katy and her children?
4. What is the problem from the client's point of view?
5. How is defensiveness demonstrated in this case study, and how might it be managed?
6. What does resistance mean in this scenario, and how might it be managed?
7. How might communication problems effectively be bridged?
8. What resources exist in your health care setting for providing culturally appropriate support to this family?
9. Because asking about insurance or payment for services is legitimate, how might such exchanges be structured to retain the personal integrity of all involved?

Case 8: A Practice Situation Involving Ethnicity

Mrs. Sophia Papadopolus is a bilingual, second-generation Greek-American who has retained a traditional Greek orientation toward family and children. Although Greek-Americans tend to be more individualistic than collective (Kourvetaris, 1978), the Greek subcommunity, of which the church is the core, is very important to Mrs. Papadopolus. Fond of saying that her grandparents came from Athens, Greece, and her parents from Athens, Georgia, she proudly claims that each generation has remained "as Greek as the last." However, her traditional Greek pride in individual achievement (Welts, 1982) led to concern about whether her teenage children will be motivated to maintain that identity with the same intensity. Of particular concern is her eldest child, a daughter, whom she suspects may not be willing to "live at home until she is properly married."

"But Greek families are very close," muses Mrs. Papadopolus, "I'm sure she'll come around."

The youngest of Mrs. Papadopolus' three children is autistic, which has been very difficult for the family, although the ethnic community has been generally supportive. Her other son, still in high school, according to Mrs. Papadopolus, is "going to go to medical school, you'll see." Her daughter, the eldest, is expected to get married, and is anticipated to do so prior to any marriage plans for her brother. Mrs. Papadopolus has definite plans for her two older children. Her husband, Yannis, although acknowledged as the master and final authority in the family, does not dispute them as long as the family honor remains intact. Mrs. Papadopolus is much more vague about the future of her autistic son, who lives at home and is cared for there by his mother and grandmother. During conversation with Mrs. Papadopolus about her children, the therapist notes that Mrs. Papadopolus somehow associates her Cypriot husband's betathalassemia trait with their son's autism. The therapist decides to investigate this more fully.

Mrs. Papadopolus is in the hospital for a hysterectomy. She is quite concerned about the surgery, the outcome in terms of her femininity, and the "gossip in the village" about her condition. She stated that she felt "fulfilled by being a mother," but questioned her continued capacity as a "wife" (that is, sexual companion) after the required surgery.

Questions for Consideration and Discussion

1. What is the problem from the client's point of view?
2. What is the problem from your point of view?
3. How would this situation be effectively managed if no health care provider of Greek descent is available? Where might the culturally sensitive and skillful provider begin?
4. What is the potential for defensiveness and resistance in this case?
5. How would those phenomena be avoided, recognized, or minimized?
6. In what areas is intervention indicated?
7. In what areas is intervention needed?
8. How might care be initiated?
9. What reactions might be anticipated in response to intervention?

Case 9: A Practice Situation Involving Beliefs[3]

Several patients from the oncology clinic were having coffee in the cafeteria while they waited for the clinic to open for their group session. Conversations ranged from personal ailments and progress to exercise techniques and diet among the African-American, two European-Americans, Korean, and Puerto Rican members of the group who were present. When one of the European-Americans mentioned a dream she had the night before, the Korean quickly stopped her with an explanation that the listeners would have "bad things" happen to them if they heard a dream recounted during daylight hours. He continued, if the contents of the dream were positive and it was shared during daylight hours, it might be only the dreamer who would have bad luck and the listeners might have good luck. But if the contents of the dream were bad, they were ensured that all would have bad luck. On the other hand, if the dream was shared during nighttime hours, both the dreamer and the listeners would be protected.

There were several puzzled faces around the table. Finally the African-American, a retired professor, remarked, "That sounds pretty far fetched to us today, Mr. Park. Where did you get that?" The Korean's reply was, "From my grandmother. She knows many things. Very real things." The European-American woman with the dream that had prompted this interaction asked if Mr. Park's grandmother knew about palm reading. It was asserted that she had and that she had imparted the rudiments of that knowledge to her grandson, who then offered to read the palms of the group present. Despite several comments about the "ridiculousness" of the situation, all consented.

Questions for Consideration and Discussion

1. How do beliefs affect behavior?
2. Why might even skeptical individuals participate in a practice such as the one described in this scenario?
3. What is the likelihood that traditional beliefs will have a negative impact on health outcome?

Case 10: A Practice Situation Involving Several Variables

Maxie is an African-American RN who works as charge nurse at the university medical center and has just been told by a medical intern that the refrigerator in which the medical students and interns store urine specimens until they test them is in need of cleaning. "That refrigerator is used only by the students and interns," Maxie explained, "The nurses don't use it." The intern shrugged and left the unit.

Two days later the intern again approached Maxie about the condition of the refrigerator, asking why it had not been cleaned. "I explained to you the other day, Doctor, that the nurses are not responsible for that refrigerator. You might mention it to housekeeping." The intern responded with, "Maxie, do you really think that you are too good to clean that refrigerator?"

Questions for Consideration and Discussion

1. What is going on in this interaction?
2. What aspects of Maxie's social status have influenced the exchanges between Maxie and the intern? For example, what influence have gender, occupation, educational level, and ethnicity on the situation? What additional variables may influence the circumstances described?
3. What assumptions might the intern be making about Maxie's circumstances?
4. In your analysis of this scenario, did you assume that the intern was male? Was it assumed that Maxie was female? Would it matter? If so, how or why?

Case 11: A Practice Situation Involving Age and Ethnicity[4]

Edward is a 10-year-old boy from Nigeria, Africa, who recently underwent serious thoracic surgery. Although still on a ventilator and sedated, he was fairly awake. He nodded appropriately and squeezed his caretaker's hand. His physician and primary nurse were amazed at how well behaved and tolerant he was. Most of the children his age thrashed and fought if they were that awake. His mother explained to them that "Edward is a good boy; he will not fight." She said that he understood that the doctors and nurses were helping him and that he would "tolerate everything."

Although Edward was awake and quiet, he was medicated for pain regularly until one of the evening nurses decided that he had been so "good" all day that he did not need so much medication. He then became more restless and agitated. Asked by the primary nurse why Edward had not received more analgesic, the other nurse explained her objections to overmedicating children. The primary nurse then explained the family and cultural expectations for stoicism that Edward was attempting to meet.

Questions for Consideration and Discussion

1. What is a likely reason for resistance to medicating when acute distress is not demonstrated?
2. What nursing and medical precautions could be employed to minimize the risk of unnecessary pain?
3. What patterned variations have been observed in the ways in which people handle pain?
4. What assumptions was the evening nurse making about Edward and about children in general?

Case 12: A Practice Situation Involving a Health Condition

Janet looked at her tiny daughter and burst into tears. She wondered if she or both of them were going to die. She amended the thought, "I wonder when I will die. What is it like? How will it be?"

Janet and little Jennifer had just returned from the lab at the clinic. The results were clear: Janet was HIV+. She had gone there to be tested after a discussion about AIDS in her Alcoholics Anonymous (AA) meeting. She had never heard of anyone she knew getting AIDS. "Not out here in the suburbs . . . not women . . . not people who don't shoot up," she mused. It just did not happen; it was not possible. She had not even thought about getting Jennifer tested; she continued to push that possibility out of her mind. It had seemed so unlikely that it could ever happen to her, thought Janet. Yet if there was any risk at all, her counselor had prodded, "just go and get tested." She had, and now she was sorry.

She wondered whom she could tell; not her mother or her sister, that was for sure. Could she tell the AA leader or the counselor at the church? Maybe. She didn't know. First she had to know more about what it meant. Did being "HIV+" mean you had AIDS? How close were they to being the same? At the clinic they had said they were different, but Janet was too upset to remember how, even if she had understood it at the time.

Janet wiped her eyes, fastened Jennifer into her car seat, and pulled away from the curb. Preoccupied, she did not pay the usual amount of attention to the lights on the way home. She did not see the speeding pick-up, overloaded with truck tires, until it hit the car. The paramedics were efficient and the ambulance sped its way to the emergency room at Valley Central. There an assistant, finding Janet unable to provide the necessary information, opened her purse in search of identification. With her wallet was the slip from the clinic with the HIV result.

Questions for Consideration and Discussion

1. How is the knowledge of Janet's condition likely to affect how she is handled at Valley Central or any other facility?
2. What is likely to change in the provider-client relationship when it is known that someone is HIV+?
3. What are the implications for provider roles? (Be careful not to limit those to physical factors.)
4. What is likely to be at the root of resistance to caring for persons living with HIV or AIDS?
5. How might stereotyping, dehumanizing interaction occur?

Nate: A Practice Situation
Involving Institutionalized Racism[5]

Nate is a tall, thin, 12-year-old African American boy in the sixth grade in a private school. Prior to his enrollment at Gregory Jefferson School three years ago, Nate went to a public elementary school where he tested well but did not achieve academically. His mother, Louise, decided that the discipline associated with private schools might help Nate improve his grades and study habits. Louise prioritizes an education for Nate that will maximize his opportunities to get a "good-paying, white-collar job."

Louise, a baccalaureate graduate, is the educational coordinator of a local program for youth job training. Louise frequently comments that she does not want Nate to become one of the troubled and unpromising youth she deals with at work. Nate, on the other hand, considers his mother "overprotective." Nate's parents are divorced. His father, with whom Nate has an ambivalent relationship, has remarried and has several other children. He visits Nate about once a month.

Two years ago Louise lost her job due to layoffs. With her current position, her annual income is reduced from $18,000 to $13,500. During the same time period Louise experienced the death of a significant other as well as physical problems that led to major abdominal surgery.

Although Louise's pay is theoretically adequate to cover the family's educational and living expenses, she tends to overspend on consumer goods. For the past two years Louise has been consistently late in paying the tuition at Gregory Jefferson School. Now she is two semesters in arrears, although she has promised to pay the tuition with her income tax return (which, last year, she did).

It is school policy that teachers do not officially communicate with parents whose children's tuition is significantly overdue. "Not communicating" with parents includes not sending report cards, therefore parents are dependent on teachers' informal notes and children's self-reports of how and what they are doing in school. When Nate's academic performance dropped off significantly, his teacher gave him several notes to take home to his mother. Unknown to either adult, the notes remained crumpled in the recesses of his desk. When Louise contacted the school for information, she was met with requests for payment.

Although the Gregory Jefferson School population is predominately African American, its administration is European American. About half of the teachers are black and half are white. Nate's teacher, Rebecca Radcliff, is a white woman in her late fifties. Long familiar with the school, Rebecca's own children attended Gregory Jefferson years ago. Recently Rebecca experienced a difficult time putting her mother into a nursing home in another state.

This week Nate was suspended from school for 3 days (after two warnings) due to his hair cut, a flat top with shaven sides and double razor etching. The suspension upset Nate (as well as his closest friend and classmate, Stan) because some other students had cuts similar to Nate's and were not suspended. The school has a policy that males must have short hair (although the principal's is of medium length). Nate initially said that he did not have the money for another haircut, but then got it from his father when he visited. He did not tell his mother about the suspension, or that he had skipped school an additional day as well. Nate skips school often and is clearly failing in all of his subjects. When he is there, however, he feels (and Stan concurs) that he is the focus of negativity by Rebecca Radcliff. Nate has been used as an example of lack of motivation in the classroom and has been predicted to fail "as he has in the past." He says that he has also been called "stupid" by the teacher.

Nate's response to the negativism he experiences has been to give up. At home he spends most of his time shut-up in his room. He no longer does his homework or turns in assignments. He does not study or participate actively in class. When Lisa Johnson, the health care provider doing a residency at Gregory Jefferson School, noticed during routine health assessments of the sixth graders that the health form completed by Nate's mother noted a 3-year history of asthma and that Nate was marked frequently absent, the family was contacted. For the past 3 years Nate's mother has believed that he has asthma. Louise attributed the asthma to bronchitis in infancy and stated that it was still a "real problem." When she gets angry with him, he has an attack, to which she responds by retracting whatever punishment or criticism she previously gave him. She also allows him to skip school when he is "ill."

At school, attempts to assess the situation were met with descriptions by the teacher and the principal of Nate as lazy, a failure, "a total loss," and a philanderer. The latter descriptor was based on his father's reputation as a womanizer; Nate was not sexually active at the time. He was also characterized as "getting ready to be one more black man standing on a street corner." No respiratory symptoms were included in the characterization, and neither the principal nor Nate's teacher believed Nate had asthma. He was not being followed medically, although the condition was diagnosed by a physician in the past.

An Analysis of Nate's Case

An in-depth analysis of Nate's situation is provided as a model for analysis of other scenarios. In considering how you would initiate an interaction with Nate or analyze Nate's situation, try to avoid speculation related to information that is not provided about Nate's circumstances. The scenario is reported here very much as it transpired. Other decisions could have been made and other approaches tried, however, which would have resulted in different situations worthy of discussion and additional analysis.

To start a conversation, the choice of a "safe" topic might lead to asking how Nate feels and following with, for example, "Nate, tell me about your asthma . . ." An open-ended approach such as that is valuable because it allows the broadest range of responses and avoids leading Nate into areas about which he might feel defensive or into answers expected or suggested by the questioner.

Nate answered the query by describing asthma as a "breathing sickness." He said that he coughed and wheezed when he exerted himself, but stated that "It only bothers me when I play basketball." The provider responded to Nate's answer by investigating further Nate's sports interests and activities, his symptoms and symptom alleviation strategies, and his beliefs about asthma. In response to those inquiries, Nate stated that asthma led him to feel different from his friends and to minimize his activity because he might have trouble breathing. He stated that his symptoms did not occur every time he exerted himself, that he had not been seen by a doctor for about 6 months, that he had never required theophylline or hospitalization, that his inhaler was empty, and that his mother "hung over" him too much, which he felt also provoked his attacks.

Continued interaction with Nate involved asking him if he was interested in learning about asthma so that he could lead a more active life. His response was positive, although he expressed surprise that asthmatics could be active in sports. When Nate was asked if there were any other areas in which he could use assistance, he reiterated that he would like his mother to "baby" him less. Lisa, the provider, told Nate that she would contact his mother to discuss the issues that he had brought to her attention. She also decided to have another discussion with Nate's teacher.

The provider contacted Nate's mother and arranged a meeting. Prior to the date set to meet his mother, Nate's teacher, Rebecca, again communicated skepticism about his having even mild, chronic asthma and added that he skipped school so often that he was failing. Further discussion, prompted by Rebecca's obvious disapproval of Nate and hopelessness for his situation, led to her disclosure of the tuition and other problems. At that point Lisa questioned her own role as a health care provider in what appeared to be a conflictual relationship between the school and Nate's parent. Realizing that Nate needed help and given the goal of assessing the situation and delineating a plan for intervention and evaluation, however, she persisted.

Assessment

Assessment and analysis of assessment data involve sifting through information to identify and understand patterns, interrelationships, and meanings assigned to various aspects of the data. Whether or not it is consciously acknowledged, we continually analyze or assign meaning to information. The meanings assigned are shaped by past experiences, cultural orientations, professional expectations, and a variety of other influences of which we may be only partially aware. It must be kept in mind that assessment and interpretation are never totally objective. They help create and shape the facts, innuendoes and inferences that are important to the application of the problem solving process.

Some analysis is ongoing and occurs in the "here and now" of a given situation; some follows a given interaction as the result of a deliberate process of assigning meaning to information. In either case, the cultural assessment must be placed in context (Jacobsen, 1988). Disclosure of interrelationships, providing literature support for interpretations, application of appropriate theory, and models all serve to clarify the issues and elucidate the presence of gaps in information. Such review and analysis sets the stage for and guides actual intervention.

To analyze Nate's situation, it is recommended that Articulation Triangles be utilized to assist with understanding the problem from the point of view of each participant (Figures 3.1, 3.2, 3.3). Before the impact of those can be comprehended in sensitive and knowledgeable ways, it is crucial to understand how the interactive processes of negative stigmatization and labeling work to create and maintain subordinate statuses. Consider how and to what extent the choices, decisions, and behaviors of each participant might affect the others and themselves. Literature is often useful to document or support

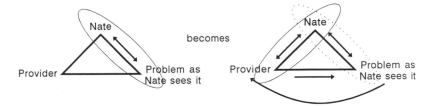

Figure 3.1.

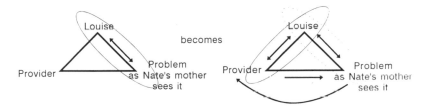

Figure 3.2.

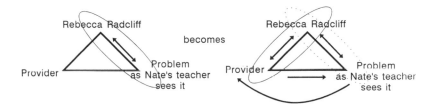

Figure 3.3. Client-Provider (Figures 3.1, 3.2, 3.3)

interpretations and to apply a theoretical framework to the information. Various analytical models, such as the Interactive Decision Model (Figure 3.4) may help to ascertain relationships and interactive processes.

There are several broad areas of problems and issues that are readily apparent upon analysis of the behaviors that have impact in this case study. For example, communication patterns, including disrespect and jeopardized personal integrity and social support; use of power; long-term consequences of the situation as it is affected by race and policy; financial strain and coping patterns; and a variety of defensive behaviors, stereotypes, and assumptions are appropriate selections for particular attention in Nate's case.

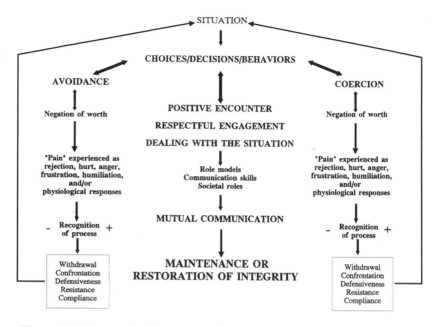

Figure 3.4. Interactive-Decision Model

Communication Patterns

Communication problems are evident between Louise and Nate (mother and son) and the family and school (Nate and Louise, teacher and principal). It is readily apparent that Nate is the individual on whom these communication problems are likely to have the greatest impact and who stands to be most hurt by them. The patterns of communication that were described inhibit effective mother-son communication. They also threaten to compromise Nate's opportunity for an education and his development of the ability to communicate meaningfully with others, including those in authority. Additionally, they reinforce Nate's inadequate coping mechanisms, that is, his avoidance of dealing directly with the issues.

People often do not realize the kinds of impressions that they convey (DePaulo, Kenny, Hoover, Webb, & Oliver, 1987). Consequently, both verbal and nonverbal communicative behavioral patterns require elucidation. Attention to the content of exchanges, underlying themes or agenda, delivery patterns, pauses and silences, and omissions contributes to analysis of verbal patterns. Nonverbal starting points include, among others, comfort levels of the participants, perception and reception of the health care provider by the other participants, and the congruence of communication.

The meanings behind Nate's behaviors and the messages to which Nate is responding deserve attention. Nate is not listened to. What he thinks and feels is not viewed as important. Nate becomes a nonentity, invisible in the situation. Nonetheless, he remains passively responsive. By giving up, Nate is ensuring a negative response from the school. He has also learned that he can get what he wants from his mother if he is "ill," so he uses asthma to help avoid issues. However, Nate is a normal child who wants to please, until he becomes convinced that is not possible.

The lack of a support system leaves Nate with inadequate sources of positive feedback. When Nate feels bad, he has no one to share that with. When he attends school, Nate has Stan, but their interaction is limited by the structured school environment in which attempts to extend direct communication time may get both boys "in trouble." To be near Stan, Nate must risk Rebecca Radcliff's negativism, and Stan is unavailable when Nate skips school. Nate has neither outlets nor opportunity to break out of his chain of behaviors. He channels his frustration into anger, largely at himself, as he moves closer to the teacher and principal's self-fulfilling prophecy.

In Nate's case, a number of factors influence the communication patterns. For example, there is the experience of lacking an African-American male role model at home and school, Louise's economic and parenting pressures (including limited knowledge of normal patterns of growth and development), the school's need and demand for payment, a tendency to focus on pathology and the negative, and a variety of stereotypes. The outcomes and consequences, both immediate and long-term, of each behavior are important.

Use of Power

There are significant power differentials in Nate's situation. He and his mother have devised several means of controlling each other, although Nate still feels overcontrolled by his parent. Both Nate and Louise, when the specifics of Nate's academic circumstances are considered, are subordinate to his teacher and the principal of the school.

When individuals differ in some way from those in power (for example, being male in a female-dominated situation or vice versa, being a member of an ethnic or racial minority group, being poor in an affluent society, being elderly in a youth-oriented society, or experiencing any other minority status), there are issues that are related to those differences.

Avoidance of dealing with potentially painful situations maintains the power of those who already have it and reinforces the minority status of those without power (Bowser & Hunt, 1981). There is a tendency to attribute responsibility for such situations to the minority status individuals or groups (Lum, 1986; Beck et al., 1984; Sundeen, Stuart, Rankin, & Cohen, 1985). That process constitutes "blaming the victim." Powerless, Nate has been cast in the role of "scapegoat," which is used to control or exclude "undesirables" (Scheflen, 1972; Pinderhughes, 1982). Because his behavior is not at the root of the problem, however, censure of it is not likely to resolve it (Scheflen, 1972).

Often the pain that is experienced in inequitable situations in which insensitive behaviors have occurred is traceable to differences in knowledge about the situation. That is, insensitivity may be the result of limited understanding of the situation rather than of intent to hurt or discriminate. Persons in positions of power often do not perceive a need to understand the issues (Berreman, 1962). For example, the issue of race in Nate's life may be viewed by members of the majority population as unimportant or may not be acknowledged as an issue at all. This is particularly likely to happen when it is easier or more comfortable to view it as a non-issue. It has often been said, according to Terry (1981), that "to be white in America is not to have to think about it" (p. 120). Many Americans have that luxury. Those who are not "white" do not. Nate is one of those, because race in America remains very much a real issue in terms of experiential differences. Generally, African-Americans perceive significantly more discrimination than European-Americans think occurs (Sigelman & Welch, 1991)

Persons in subordinate statuses experience the consequences of the issue. In search for personal integrity in a sometimes inhospitable environment and to survive, they learn more about the issue(s) and to make sense out of their worlds. For example, when personal value is attached to categories of stratification (for example, economic class or race), persons and groups who fall into lesser stratifications may respond by accommodation to the imposed expectations (that is, they may fulfill the self-fulfilling prophecy), or they may respond assertively and resist the stigma associated with the categories in which they are socially categorized (Woldemikael, 1987).

One way of asserting resistance to stereotypic expectations is to manipulate identity to narrow the gaps between the powerful and the less powerful, that is, between the minority and majority statuses (Berreman, 1962, Foster & White, 1982). When the characteristics on which categorization is based are unchangeable, as is skin color, it is more difficult to manipulate identity. In the case of Nate, however, Louise has attempted to do it by presenting herself and Nate as financially stable, middle-class consumers. The principal and teacher, assuming that the apparent resources were real, did not understand the financial strain experienced by the family.

Issues are problematic because they are experienced as discomforting. As a result of the unsettled or uncomfortable connotations associated with "touchy" issues, they tend to be avoided. For that reason, in American society, issues related to racial differences are frequently avoided. To defend against discomfort, emphasis on the issue will be minimized and the issue made as invisible as possible. Persons associated with the issue may also become "invisible." As unintended pain caused by insensitivity increases the responsibility to avoid insensitive behaviors increase. However, it follows that there is also responsibility to deal with issues whose avoidance compromises personal and group integrity and perpetuates opportunities for harm to occur. When individuals with minority status are treated as if differences do not exist or are not important, the minority individual experiences pain. The majority individual can ignore the situation, the minority individual cannot—whether or not the situation or consequent pain is intentional.

In Nate's case, the result of the school's not dealing with his academic failure is that he is denied the opportunity to learn more effective coping mechanisms. The situation demonstrates how school personnel take from Nate the opportunity for upward mobility and expose him to negative stereotyping. This sets up Nate for victimization through the process of "self-fulfilling prophecy." It is an obstacle to Nate's perceiving that he is okay.

Consequences: An Onus of Race

In interaction among peoples of differing national, cultural, ethnic, racial, class and/or other origins, classificatory phenomena have different meanings for each group and individual involved (Woldemikael, 1987). Given the many and varied interpretations of past and present circumstances, and the uneven incorporation of minority groups into American society, racially integrated situations often lead to increased stress and lowered self esteem (Albrecht, Thomas, & Chadwick, 1980).

In addition to his personal experiences, Nate has a history based on his ethnic and socioeconomic background. He knows not only intellectually, but also from television and personal observations that blacks are often perceived negatively. He has a good chance of interpreting the connection between money and personal worth in a way somewhat similar to this: "Since Mom doesn't have money, she is not respected by the school. If Mom is not respected, neither am I. The school treats me and my mom as worthless." Generally society does not demonstrate sensitivity to the history of blacks and their devaluation as slave "property," or to the cultural and psychological "baggage" left by that heritage (Jaynes & Williams, 1989; Sigelman & Welch, 1991).

African American adolescents, in particular black males (Leavy, 1983) are "endangered" (Gibbs, 1984), that is, they are vulnerable to epidemic rates of unemployment, substance abuse, illiteracy, teenage parenthood, and mortality by suicide, homicide, and accidents. Unskilled, unemployed, and undereducated, many enter adulthood without skills or attitudes and experiences that will encourage development of occupations and upward mobility. This frequently leads to cycles of poverty and disenfranchisement. This process, in sum, exemplifies the institutionalized discrimination which, when race and class are combined, results commonly in underachievement (Carmichael & Hamilton, 1968; Milner, 1983; Jaynes & Williams, 1989).

Social inequality and stratification are cultural traits. Interactions that generate and maintain those phenomena are learned and socially transmitted, and are, therefore, subject to change. Overlooking or ignoring such phenomena perpetuates institutionalized inequalities and inhibits potentially productive interpersonal exchanges.

In ethnically stratified societies such as the United States, with its two-category, that is, white/non-white system (Daniels & Kitano, 1970), a minority individual's chances may be strongly affected by his or her specific ethnic category. Advances in the physical and social sciences, with the redefinition of race as a social rather than biological phenomenon, have left racist themes of inherent inferiority untenable. Racism remains, however, a significant factor in social process, social organization, and culture (Bowser & Hunt, 1981; Geller, 1988; Jaynes & Williams, 1989; Steinberg, 1989; Sigelman & Welch, 1991). Denying the significance of that situation implies that specific experiences of individuals and groups are not important.

Consequences: An Onus of Policy

The effects of the policy of the school's not communicating with Louise are also important. The messages sent to Nate and Louise by the school's policies include that the school prioritizes money over this student. Nate learns that the school cares less about his academic progress and success than about his accommodation to the social expectation of tuition payment. (In justice to the school's position, tuition is necessary to maintain the organization.) By failing to pay their bill, Nate and Louise are socially ostracized from the society of the school and no longer "deserve" or qualify for communication, although the school has avoided open acknowledgment of the situation. An association is likely to be made, however, between money and personal worth. Without money, one is treated differently and is without power.

Another problem is that Nate is wasting time at Gregory Jefferson School, yet no effort has been made to relocate him. That situation moves Nate closer to the self-fulfilling prophecy.

Louise, like increasing numbers of parents (Clark, 1980), has used the school to absorb some of her parenting and socializing responsibilities. The school, however, rejects that role because Louise has not kept her contract, that is, paid the tuition.

Consider what Nate's principal's and teacher's attitudes, the school's policy, his mother's communication and parenting styles, and his teacher's communication and teaching styles have in common. None of those deal directly with Nate as a person with adolescent needs. They present several examples of avoidance. The responses of the school's personnel and policy, however, push Nate into a corner. That is an example of coercion.

Avoidance of direct encounter with the problem may imply additional issues. For example, dependence on policy as a rationale for behavior allows avoidance of the sense of guilt that many European Americans share about having ancestors who were responsible for the limited status, power, and wealth that African Americans had in the past and many still face today.

Stereotypes and Assumptions

There are a number of stereotypes and assumptions involved in Nate's situation. Stereotypes involve categorical evaluation of someone according to race, gender, ethnicity, or other classification (for example, "good doctor," "male nurse," or "black professor") with implications based on characteristics associated with the group described (Fiske, 1989). Stereotypes are most likely to be used when an individual can be pointed out as different, is alone, or is one of few in an otherwise homogeneous environment (Fiske, 1989). Like images frozen in time, stereotypes deny diversity among people in a group.

Some of the stereotypes relevant to Nate's situation are included in the right hand column of Table 3.1, with an analysis of the consequences of specified behaviors.

Social Process Issues
in the Preceding Assessment and Analysis

While attitudes toward minority statuses are generally less negative than they were in the past (Jones, 1981), many Americans exhibit relative complacence regarding ethnic, racial, cultural, and gender issues (Steinberg, 1989). Personal avoidance of interethnic or interracial confrontations tends to be mistakenly equated with freedom from prejudice and discrimination.

Avoidance functions in interactive contexts as a short term safeguard of smooth interpersonal relations. However, because belief in the validity of traits such as those commonly associated with ethnicity

(text continues on p. 115)

Table 3.1 Analysis of Nate's Situation

Behavior	Issues	Stereotypes & Assumptions
Decision to put Nate in private school	Association of public schools with failure and lack of opportunity: avoidance of failure	"Private is better." Separation from black group is insurance that Nate will turn out acceptable to society at large. Louise has done her part by providing private school.
Priority goal for Nate: "good-paying, white-collar" job	Wanting "more" for Nate. "White-collar" jobs pay more money and command more status in our society. Nate's mother is determined not to use Nate's father as a role model. Others who are black and male and positive role models, however, are not available to Nate. Nate is set up for a self-fulfilling prophecy because he is not getting the foundation he needs to accomplish the goal of getting a good job and because he, as a black male, shares some commonalities with his "rejectable" father.	Louise has fulfilled her parenting role by enrolling Nate at Gregory Jefferson School. Nate's father (who does not have a job) is inadequate as an adult, a man, and a parent.
£, § Teacher punishes Nate for his academic and behavioral inadequacies. School and teacher mistreat Nate with negative behavior and by wasting his time there.	*, £, § Scapegoating and blaming the victim. *, § The punishment does not match the situation. Eventually, the school will have its payment, but Nate will still not have an education and will have lost a year of normal opportunity.	"Black males are shiftless and irresponsible." Nate's haircut represents to the teacher and principal an unacceptable symbol of his identity (that is, one of rebellion).
Other expenses may have priority over	Desire for immediate gratification and respect	Status is gained through conspicuous consump-

(continued)

Table 3.1 (Continued)

Behavior	Issues	Stereotypes & Assumptions
tutition.	in a consumption-oriented society. £ Denial of realistic financial ability.	tion. Love equals things.
£, § Having school policy that teachers do not communicate with parents whose children's tuition is not paid.	*, £, § Institutional power and control *, § Correlation of money with personal worth. *, £, § Scapegoating and blaming the victim. #, £ Individual is not the priority.	It is the victim's fault. The bill could be paid; the resources exist but Louise is holding back. Wealth = worth. Poor people need not or should not have valued and attractive things, particularly if bills are not paid.
£, § School suspends Nate.	*, £, § Institutional power and control: Parent feels powerless against the authority of the school. *, £, § Scapegoating and blaming the victim.	Nate is not worth further investment by the school.
£ Nate does not tell his mother about the suspension, his hooking school, and his failing grades.	£ Self-protection and avoidance of Louise's anger, as well as his own guilt. Louise avoids by denying evidence of school problems because she feels that she has done all that she can.	Negative communication: "No news is good news." Children do not require active parenting; they grow and develop by themselves in their teen years. Other time-consuming aspects of life (such as earning a living) are more crucial than parenting.
Nate's friend Stan tells the health care provider that Nate is being treated unfairly and harshly.	Peer support: * Stan recognizes that Nate is being victimized. Stereotypically, however, children are powerless and not listened to.	Nate is important.

Table 3.1 Continued

Behavior	Issues	Stereotypes & Assumptions
§ Louise handles Nate's asthma as a serious factor in mother-son relationship.	§ Beliefs about illness. § Explanatory model. £,^ Beliefs about sick role behaviors, parental role, and that love for a sick child means reduced expectations of him or her. £ Chronic illness releases Nate from expectations of productivity in his view and in his mother's. £ Dependence on illness as an excuse broadens the gap between school and family, as well as between the family members themselves. Louise's avoidance of providing treatment for Nate's asthma enables both Nate and Louise to perpetuate their ineffective pattern of communication and behavior.	Asthma is debilitating. Illness releases one from normal responsibilities. It is better to be sick than an academic failure.
£, § School deals with Nate's behavior from its own perspective, which coincides with predominant societal view.	*, £, § Perpetuation of a system in which blacks are often expected to produce little and to have limited opportunities. Does the school want to prove black males' strengths or weaknesses? Self-fulfilling prophecy.	Black males are poor investments. As limited producers, they represent a "throw away" part of society. Furthermore, they are seen as threatening, so are not worthy of investment, respect, and support.
*, £ Choice by teacher and principal not to invest further in Nate.	*, £ Institutional power and control using policy to justify rejection of Nate. The individual is not really important.	Black males are poor investments. As limited producers they are a "throw away" part of society.

(Continued)

Table 3.1 Continued

Behavior	Issues	Stereotypes & Assumptions
§ Teacher and principal share negative assessment of Nate with health care provider.	*, £, § Sharing of control by those in authority, who assume they can influence the health care provider's perceptions of Nate and that the health care provider will submit to the school's authority and definition of the situation and will behave accordingly. *, §, £ Stereotyping. *Self-fulfilling prophecy and disrespect for Nate.	The European-American health care provider can and will further justify the school's policy. Low-income people are not good verbalizers, do not defer gratification, are uncooperative, and are not amenable to change (Lorion & Parron, 1985).
£ Nate gives up. He does not try to achieve academically.	£ Hopelessness: Loss of personal integrity and compromised sense of self confidence.	Self-fulfilling prophecy: "Black males are irresponsible. They must be kept in check."
Health care provider works with Nate and Louise as a family/client.	Academic failure and poor self image. *, £, §, ^ Asthma: Nate does not have a working inhaler and does not have medical attention. Because asthma is exertion-induced, lack of an inhaler and medicine keep Nate inactive and close to home and to Louise. Health care provider deals with asthma through education and referral. Parenting: provider encourages Louise to allow Nate to practice decision-making within a controlled environment and helps her understand interrelationships among	Nate is at risk for victimization through self-fulfilling prophecy. Multiple levels of intervention are indicated.

Table 3.1 Continued

Behavior	Issues	Stereotypes & Assumptions
	Nate's rebellion against authority, his manipulation of somatic phenomena, and his powerlessness at school.	

NOTES: * Indicates inequity as the consequence of use of power
£ Indicates avoidance
§ Indicates coercion
# Whether or not this indicates inequity depends upon a specific community's orientation
    toward groups or individuals
^Nate's use of his asthma represents both avoidance (of his mother's anger) and coercion (by
influencing her perception of the situation)

are perpetuated through everyday communication and behavior (Phinney & Rotheram, 1987; van Dijk, 1987), avoidance condones institutionally racist aspects of society (Bowser & Hunt, 1981). Foremost among those processes are prejudice and discrimination, that is, negative attitudes and behaviors directed toward members of socially distinct collectives. Frequently, discrimination is institutionalized, with subtle barriers built into social processes that individuals unknowingly help to perpetuate.

Intervention

Members of various health care disciplines will interpret the evidence, prioritize needs, and propose intervention strategies in different ways and with varying outcomes. Regardless of professional orientation, however, in considering intervention plans, it is crucial to appraise potential positive and negative, short- and long-term outcomes of various interventions.

Intervention is actually initiated during the interaction, whether or not an analysis and plan have been formalized. It involves all aspects of interaction, communication, and the use of self. An important aspect of intervention is the inclusion of the client and family members. Inclusion involves more than presenting options from which choices are selected and, depending on the culture and situation, "family" and other persons of authority may not be blood relatives. Additionally, clients and family expectations and customs surrounding involvement in health care matters vary widely. Clients' values and views as well as professional judgment should dictate who is involved and how they are involved in health care.

Analysis of Nate's situation suggested numerous areas of potential intervention. Among those were communication with his mother, his developing identity, his peer relationships and support system, structural and organizational influences on his underachievement, and various strengths and weaknesses. Other, overlapping areas of potential intervention involved Nate's mother, Louise. Issues involving Louise included parenting, communication with Nate, budget counseling, stress management, her communication with the teacher and principal at Gregory Jefferson School, and the discrepancy between her expectations of Nate and the experiences provided for him. Additional intervention needs involved the individuals who represented the school itself, and in particular its communication with Nate and Louise, its attitude toward parents and families with problems meeting tuition payments, and its awareness of the consequences of its policies.

Health care intervention in situations such as that presented by Nate is multifaceted, involves ongoing exploration of the rights and responsibilities of the various participants in the case, and requires careful maintenance of health care provider roles and identities. In Nate's case it was necessary to designate that role as separate from others that might involve educational or administrative school roles.

Levels of Intervention

Planning for intervention entails attention to multiple levels of involvement. The health care disciplines have focused traditionally on individuals and small groups. The trend toward population-focused and societal-level involvement is relatively recent and poses numerous intervention issues that may be met with resistance by individual practitioners. Given the scarcity of health care resources among many populations and the impact of institutionalized social processes, however, it is important that clinicians and others become comfortable with analysis on the larger, societal scale. Health care includes problem-solving at all levels because limitation to individual-level experience at times treats only symptoms and ignores problems. In that case there is no mechanism for attending to other than individual consequences of such phenomena as sexism, racism, poverty, and discrimination (Devore, 1985). Unfortunately, rather than addressing institutions, there is a tendency to blame victims.

Another strong argument for emphasis on health care at multiple levels is that clear understanding of social process helps to empower health care providers, as well as consumers. Based on that understanding, the sensitivity, awareness, knowledge, and skills of health care providers can and will, if they accept that social responsibility, impact on society.

In the scenario with Nate, some health care providers might have limited assessment and intervention to his asthma, which would avoid consideration of Nate's, Louise's, or Rebecca's views of the problem and limited opportunities for culturally appropriate psychosocial assessment, planning, and intervention. Similarly, when a provider realizes that a child such as Nate is in poor standing at school, he or she might conclude that interference in academic issues is outside the appropriate roles of health care provision. In Nate's case, such avoidance would have left Nate without an advocate at school and without means of reestablishing communication with his mother.

Additional rationalizations for minimizing involvement in Nate's case might have stemmed from a desire to avoid potential conflict between the school and Nate's mother or to avoid the risk of being perceived as aligned with or against the school and its personnel. Because Nate is black and the teacher and principal are white, the health care provider might also fear that the encounter might be taken out of context and construed as racist, or, depending on the scenario, sexist or otherwise discriminatory. Each of those decisions would have functioned to maintain the status quo, which included leaving Nate unassisted in his need for advocacy and support.

In Nate's situation, patient-centered goals for intervention in the relationships among Gregory Jefferson School and Nate and his mother might have been limited to reducing truancy and providing a more positive experience for Nate at school, or encouraging placement in an environment more conducive to continuing Nate's education. However, multilevel goals went beyond those to stimulate critical evaluation of Gregory Jefferson School's policy and its implications for students such as Nate, evaluation of teaching methods that allow negativity toward individual children, and understanding by the teacher and principal of the role they play in fulfilling their negative prophecies regarding Nate and other children.

Specific interventions involved taking advocacy positions, such as acknowledging administrative challenges while confronting the use of power to avoid and coerce, elucidating the actual messages communicated (for example to Nate and Louise), and exploring the short- and long-term consequences of various school policies.

Communication Patterns

Goals and plans for intervention had to include Nate and Louise. For example, regarding communication patterns, a short-term goal of fostering communication based on mutual respect and recognition of individual needs of mother and son was determined. A long-term goal emphasized shared expectations for Nate's education. Actual behavioral interventions explored Louise's and Nate's perceptions of their interactions and interpretation of the effect of the current communication patterns and assessment of attitudes of Nate and Louise toward members of the opposite sex (Chapman, 1988).

Various advocacy tasks were encountered. For example, Louise needed to be assisted in helping Nate to cope with the negative environment that he encountered at school and both Nate and Louise needed help in articulating their concerns alone, to each other, and to the school.

Normal Adolescent Growth and Development

Other intervention efforts focused on exploring and supplementing Louise's knowledge of normal adolescent growth and development, with emphasis on needs such as trust and privacy (the latter being prompted by Louise's dislike of Nate's keeping the door closed to his room), learning to be and being responsible, individualization, self identity, and positive self concept. It was important to explore issues specific to African American child-rearing patterns. (See, for example, Clark 1980; Hines & Boyd-Franklin, 1982; Dodson, 1988; Guthrie, 1988; Jackson, McCullough, & Gurin, 1988; Manns, 1988; Peters, 1988; and Williams, 1988.)

Self Concept and Race

Nate's developing and adolescent identity needs indicated short-term goals such as identification of positive role models to reduce negativity associated with stereotypes of black males, and exploring Louise's and Nate's attitudes toward Nate's father and their implications for Nate. Long-term goals emphasized positive self regard and pride of ethnic and racial background that can facilitate motivation toward a productive future and confidence in the ability to succeed. (See, for example, Spurlock, 1986; Comer, 1987; and Marshall, 1987.)

Actual intervention behaviors included assessment and support of peer relationships and social support resources (see Pinderhughes, 1982, Bloch, 1983, and Manns, 1988). Ethnic, racial, and cultural similarities and differences must be considered if interpersonal relationships and interaction patterns are to be understood (Gudykunst, 1986). Nate's ideas about being black and being male were explored with him. (Related, recommended literature includes, for example, Gary, 1981; Poussaint, 1982; Leavy, 1983; Staples, 1983; Gibbs, 1984; Gite, 1986; Campbell, 1987a and b; Chapman, 1988; and McAdoo, 1988.)

Nate's underachievement and relationships between Nate's behavior and motivation involved short-term goals of reducing truancy and increasing achievement behaviors on Nate's part, helping Nate to discuss the problem with Louise, and reducing negative communication at home and in the classroom. Long-term goals focused on creating a foundation that will help Nate avoid the self-fulfilling prophecy phenomenon. Actual interventions related to those goals included helping Nate to accept his strengths as well as his weaknesses; encouraging his return to school; reinforcing the idea that worth is not correlated with money or material possessions; assisting with other advocacy behaviors to facilitate positive and mutual communication between Nate and his mother and Nate and his teacher; exploring remedial opportunities for Nate to increase his motivation to return and work at school; and pointing out the process of self-fulfilling prophecy, the roles played by each individual involved, and how the trajectory can be altered.

Goal Congruence

Discussion of the gap between Louise's educational goals for Nate and her behavioral follow through, beyond placing Nate in an "acceptable" school, led to realistic goals and behavioral congruence. (See, for example, Comer, 1987; Marshall, 1987; Ogbu, 1988; and Tifft, 1989.) Nate's feelings about his experiences at school and the negativism that he perceived there were explored with the attempt to put these into clearer perspective for him. This was necessary because of a tendency for African Americans to evaluate blacks even more negatively than do European Americans (Jarmon, 1980; Dyer et al., 1989).

A variety of problem-ownership exercises and stress-management techniques were used to help Nate handle negativism without increasing his vulnerability. Both acting out and withdrawing left him vulnerable and feeling bad about himself, but effective communication skills and believing that he could disprove the negative accusations increased his confidence and positive self regard.

Asthma

Closer examination was indicated of the actual and enabling roles played by Nate's asthma. Assessment of Nate's need for medication and inhaler, and of the realistic limitations and opportunities provided by participating in basketball and track were important for empowering Nate to control his disease and for elimination of negative assumptions by others.

Additionally, asthma as a disease process, that is, the physiological and psychobiological processes, and as an illness were discussed with Nate and with Louise to put into perspective the actual limitations imposed by the condition. Also explored were alternatives for the control of asthma, decrease of the use of illness as a mechanism to achieve secondary gains, steps toward a more active, normal adolescent life-style. Each of those interventions related to a goal of demystifying the sick role. Although it was not directly pertinent to the case study involving Nate, it may be important to assess for traditional health beliefs and practices among other families (see, for example, Snow, 1983).

Louise's Coping Skills

Nate's mother, Louise, expressed feelings of being overwhelmed with the responsibilities of her job and her home life. Specific short-term intervention goals involved improving parenting skills and effective management of the relationship between home and school. Long-term goals included improved strategies for coping with single parenthood, understanding an adolescent son, a demanding job, communication, and increased congruence between expectations and resources.

Intervention behaviors emphasized referral for budget counseling and financial planning and suggestions of affordable stress management resources. Also discussed was the clarification and assessment of values and the corresponding need to prioritize and balance demands and desires with resources. The following sources are recommended for related information: Almquist, 1984; Shortridge, 1984; Wilson, 1984; Beneria & Stimpson, 1987; Brimmer, 1987; Frazier, 1987; Hare, 1987; Hill, 1987; Poussaint, 1987; Voydanoff & Majka, 1988; and Boone, 1989. The significance of and adjustment to the losses that Louise had experienced were explored. Improved communication with Nate was supported. That effort included sharing resources and knowledge, modeling and role play of mutual communication skills, and exploration of the role of asthma in the relationship between Nate and his mother.

Evaluation

Continuous evaluation and reevaluation is essential to the successful intervention and building of cultural awareness, sensitivity, knowledge, and skills. Decisions that determine reactions and responses are based on evaluation of the ongoing events in a situation. Interactive processes, whether between persons or a person and an object, depend on evaluation. In interactive processes between and among persons, evaluation occurs among all who are involved. Consequently, evaluation determines the nature and characteristics of interactions. It is the application of judgments to events that health care personnel view from their own and their disciplines' various viewpoints. The judgments represent the results of the evaluative process, and rather than to be avoided or denied as inappropriate, they are most effectively formed with as much openness and accurate information as possible (Patton, 1980).

Numerous aspects of evaluation are needed in the provision of health care. Reliability and validity of the initial and sequential assessment data, for example, require careful scrutiny. Goal formulation, planning strategies, and implementation of intervention must be examined and evaluated in specific terms. Outcomes often pose a problem because health care settings at times preclude long-term follow-up, which too often leads to acceptance of short-term goals and achievements as adequate and significant.

Collages

The following collages (pp. 123-138) have been assembled from the popular media to stimulate consideration and discussion of various issues. Part II of *Promoting Cultural Diversity: Strategies for Health Care Professionals* provided strategies for organizing practice sessions to utilize the collages.

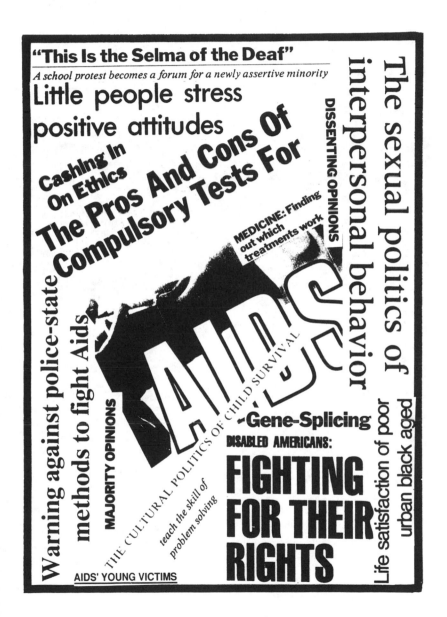

Collage 1: Ethics: Weighing Costs and Benefits

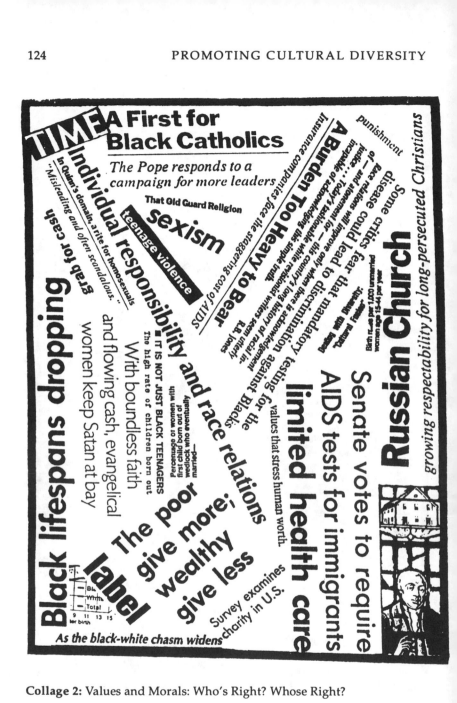

Collage 2: Values and Morals: Who's Right? Whose Right?

Packing Protection in a Purse

❝ . . . It is clear that the Community Relations Commission has not been functional for some time now and it has been a concern of mine . . . ❞

Ability grouping is under attack

Educated whites most apt to own guns

Owners of guns feel less secure at home than others, poll finds

Values education

the death of the American Dream

Socioeconomic pressure, gang activity and drugs fuel frightening trend

The rape culture

U.S. prisons' population tops 500,000

Dial-a-porn

Tiny fingers on the trigger

Tougher criminal penalties for juvenile offenders

More government spending on educational and recreational facilities for teenagers

Greater restraints on the showing of sex and violence on television

Greater restraints on the showing of sex and violence in movies

Greater restraints on sex and violence in rock-music lyrics

Holding parents legally liable for the violent criminal actions of their children

Many boys have their first sexual experience while watching sadistic slasher films at gross-out parties. By age 16, a child has seen 200,000 acts of violence on television.

■ VIOLENCE IS THE WEAPON

CHILD: INTERPRETIVE AND STRUCTURAL IMPLICATIONS OF THE MALTREATMENT OF THE BUREAUCRACY AND THE

TEENS GONE WILD

■ GRAND ILLUSION

TEENS UNDER PRESSURE

housing

Sexual harassment: The link between gender stratification, sexuality, and women's economic status

Collage 3: Social Pressure, Social Protection

Collage 4: The Price of Dichotomies: "Have's" and "Have-Nots"

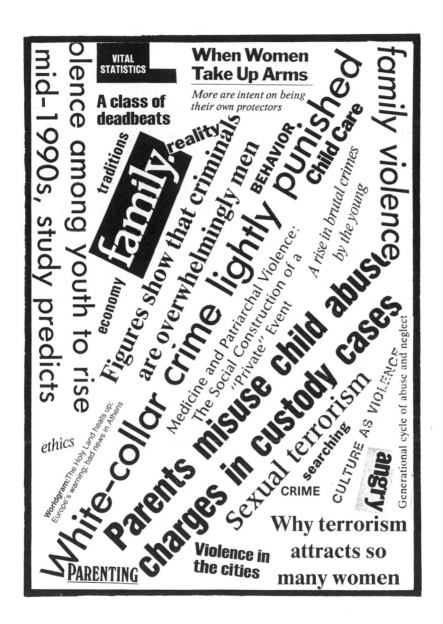

Collage 5: The Culture of Violence and the Violence of Culture

Collage 6: The Use and Abuse of Social Institutions

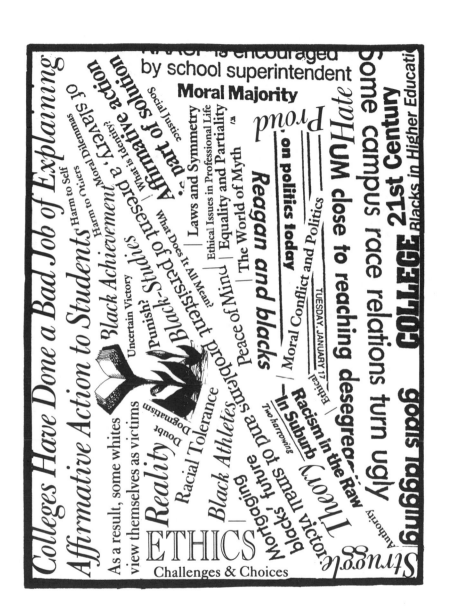

Collage 7: Race: Biological Trivia and Social Fuse

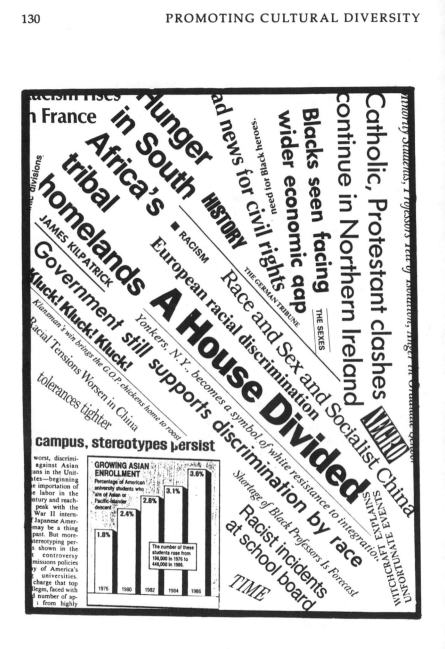

Collage 8: Compromised Development and Historical Backlash

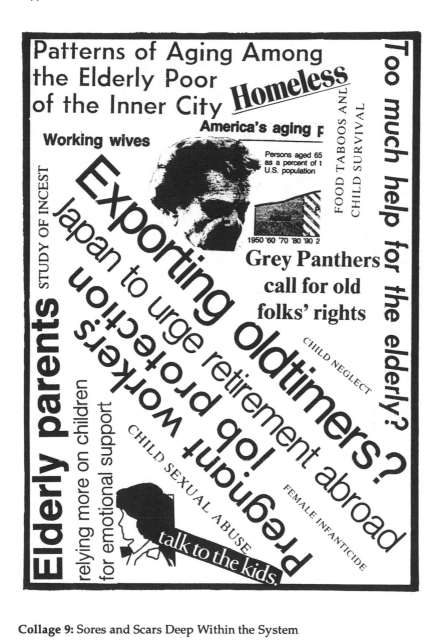

Collage 9: Sores and Scars Deep Within the System

Collage 10: Maybe Someday We Can Say, "Racism Used to Be . . . But Not Anymore"

Collage 11: The Cost of Categories: Challenge? Change? Communication?

Collage 12: Access: Civil Right or Civil Rite?

Collage 13: Man and Wo(mb)=Man and Not-Man

Collage 14: Woman's Worth: The Wedge Between Equality and Patriarchy

Collage 15: Asserting Female Values in a Male World

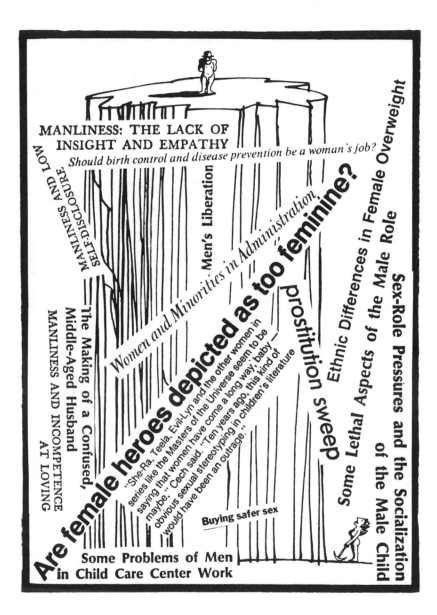

Collage 16: The Double Whammy: Taught to Adjust to a Man's World, Expected to Like It

Summary

Part III of *Promoting Cultural Diversity: Strategies for Health Care Professionals* introduced a selection of case studies and collages with which to practice the analytical and communication skills presented in Parts I and II. The case studies function as exercises that involve common areas of diversity including sex role and gender, disparity in socioeconomic status, ethnicity, age, health conditions, and race.

The final case study, a situation involving institutionalized racism, is developed to provide a detailed example of problem identification and analysis.

Notes

1. Abigail Turowski, University of Maryland—College Park, is acknowledged for her contribution to this scenario.

2. William Moore, IV, University of Maryland School of Nursing, is acknowledged for his contribution to this scenario.

3. Jacqueline Beezer, University of Maryland School of Nursing, is acknowledged for her contribution to this scenario.

4. Karen Twit, University of Maryland School of Nursing, is acknowledged for her contribution to this scenario.

5. Sharon Strobel, University of Maryland School of Nursing, is acknowledged for her contribution to this section.

References

Aboud, F. E., & Skerry, A. (1984). The development of ethnic attitudes: A critical review. *Journal of Cross-Cultural Psychology, 15*, 3-34.

Adair, J., Deuschle, K. W., & Barnett, C. R. (1988). *The people's health: Anthropology and medicine in a Navajo community*. Albuquerque: University of New Mexico Press.

Albrecht, S. L, Thomas, D. L, & Chadwick, B. A. (1980). *Social psychology*. Englewood Cliffs, NJ: Prentice-Hall.

Almquist, E. (1984). Race and ethnicity in the lives of minority women. In J. Freeman, (Ed.), *Women: A feminist perspective*. (pp. 423-453). Palo Alto, CA: Mayfield.

American Nurses' Association. (1987). *Facts about nursing 86-87*. Kansas City, MO: American Nurses' Association.

Andersen, K. (1985). Private violence: The unspeakable crimes are being yanked out of the shadows. In L. W. Barnes, (Ed.), *Social problems 85/86* (pp. 188-189). Guilford, CT: Dushkin.

Anderson, J. A. (1986, November). Conflict with learning styles. *Proceedings of the 2nd Conference on Black Student Retention in Higher Education* (pp. 80-114). Atlanta, GA: (Host) Florida Agricultural and Mechanical University.

Anderson, J. A. (1990, January). *An innovative three-level strategy for the retention of minority students*. Paper presented at a workshop offered by the Office of Student Affairs' Professional Development Program, University of Maryland at Baltimore.

Andrulis, D. P. (1977). Ethnicity as a variable in the utilization and referral patterns of a comprehensive mental health center. *Journal of Community Psychology, 5*, 231-237.

Banton, M. (1983). *Racial and ethnic competition*. Cambridge, UK: Cambridge University Press.

Bauwens, E. E. (1978). *The anthropology of health*. St. Louis: C. V. Mosby.

Beck, C. M., Rawlins, R. P., & Williams, S. R. (1984). *Mental health psychiatric nursing: A holistic life-cycle approach*. St. Louis, MO: C. V. Mosby.

Becker, H. S. (1963). *Outsiders: Studies in the sociology of deviance*. New York: Free Press of Glencoe.

Beneria, L., & Stimpson, C. R. (Eds.). (1987). *Women, households and the economy*. New Brunswick, NJ: Rutgers University Press.

Benner, P., & Wrubel, J. (1989). *The primacy of caring: Stress and coping in health and illness*. Reading, MA: Addison-Wesley.

Berreman, G. D. (1962). *Behind many masks*. Society for Applied Anthropology, Monograph No. 4. Indianapolis: Bobbs-Merrill.

Berreman, G. D. (1973). Bazaar behavior: Social identity and social interaction in urban India. In G. DeVos & L. Romanucci-Ross, (Eds.), *Ethnic identity: Cultural continuities and change* (pp. 71-105). Palo Alto, CA: Mayfield.

Berreman, G. D. (1981). *Social inequality: Comparative and developmental approaches*. New York: Academic Press.

Bidwell, A. S., & Brasler, M. L. (1989). Role modeling versus mentoring in nursing education. *Image, 21*(1), 23-25.

Bloch, B. (1983). Nursing care of black patients. In M. Orque, B. Bloch, & L. Monrroy (Eds.), *Ethnic nursing care: A multicultural approach* (pp. 81-115). St. Louis: C. V. Mosby.

Blumer, H. (1969). *Symbolic interactionism: Perspective and method*. Englewood Cliffs, NJ: Prentice-Hall.

Boone, M. S. (1982). A socio-medical study of infant mortality among disadvantaged Blacks. *Human Organization, 41*(3), 227-236.

Boone, M. S. (1989). *Capital crime: Black infant mortality in America*. Newbury Park, CA: Sage.

Bowman, R., & Culpepper, R. (1974). Power: Rx for change. *American Journal of Nursing, 74*, 1054-1056.

Bowser, B. P., & Hunt, R. G. (Eds.). (1981). *Impacts of racism on white Americans*. Beverly Hills, CA: Sage.

Boyle, J. S., & Andrews, M. M. (1989). *Transcultural concepts in nursing care*. Glenview, IL: Scott, Foresman.

Brimmer, A. F. (1987, August). Income and wealth: One of the fastest growing segments of American society since 1980, black middle class faces widening gap between well off and the poor. *Ebony*, pp. 42, 46, 48.

Brislin, R. P., & Pedersen, P. (1976). *Cross-cultural orientation programs*. New York: Gardner.

Brislin, R. W., Cushner, K., Cherrie, C., & Yong, M. (1986). *Intercultural interactions: A practical guide*. Newbury Park, CA: Sage.

Britain, G. M., & Cohen, R. (Eds.). (1980). *Hierarchy and society: Anthropological perspectives on bureaucracy*. Philadelphia: Institute for the Study of Human Issues.

Brown, E. R. (1980). *Rockefeller medicine men: Medicine and capitalism in America*. Berkeley: University of California Press.

Brownlee, A. T. (1978). *Community, culture, and care: A cross-cultural guide for health workers*. St. Louis: C. V. Mosby.

Butler, R. (1969). Age-ism: Another form of bigotry. *The Gerontologist, 9*, 243-246.

Campbell, B. M. (1987a, February). Successful women, angry men. *Ebony*, pp. 38, 40, 42, 44.

Campbell, B. M. (1987b, July). Is it true what they say about black men? *Ebony*, pp. 116, 118, 120, 122, 124.

Carmichael, S., & Hamilton, C. V. (1968). *Black power*. London, UK: Cape.

Chapman, A. B. (1988). Male-female relations: How the past affects the present. In H. P. McAdoo (Ed.), *Black families* (pp. 190-200). Newbury Park, CA: Sage.

Chien, C. (1991, Summer). Personal communication. Course, NURS 707: Health, Health Care and Culture. University of Maryland at Baltimore.

Chinn, P. L., & Wheeler, C. E. (1985). Feminism and nursing: Can nursing afford to remain aloof from the women's movement? *Nursing Outlook, 33*(2), 74-77.

Chrisman, N. J., & Maretzki, T. W. (1982). *Clinically applied anthropology: Anthropologists in health science settings*. Dordrecht, The Netherlands: D. Reidel.

Clark, A. (1980). *Culture and childrearing*. Philadelphia: F. A. Davis.

Collier, M. J., & Thomas, M. (1988). Cultural identity: An interactive perspective. In Y. Y. Kim & W. B. Gudykunst (Eds.), *Theories in interactive communication* (pp. 99-120). Newbury Park, CA: Sage.

Comer, J. P. (1987, August). Education is the way out and up. *Ebony*, pp. 61-62, 64, 66.

Cortese, A. (1990). *Ethnic ethics: The restructuring of moral theory*. Albany: The State University of New York Press.

Cross, T. (1987). *The black power imperative: Racial inequality and the politics of violence*. New York: Faulkner.

Damon, W. (1989, May 3). Learning how to deal with the new American dilemma: We must teach our students about morality and racism. *The Chronicle of Higher Education*, B1, B-2, B-3.

Daniels, R., & Kitano, H. H. L. (1970). *American racism: Exploration of the nature of prejudice*. Englewood Cliffs, NJ: Prentice-Hall.

Degner, L. F., & Russell, C. A. (1988). Preferences for treatment control among adults with cancer. *Research in Nursing & Health, 11*, 367-374.

Dennis, K. E. (1990). Patients' control and the information imperative: Clarification and confirmation. *Nursing Research, 39*, 162-166.

Dennis, K. E. (1991). Empowerment. In J. L. Creasia & B. Parker, (Eds.). *Conceptual foundations of professional nursing practice* (pp. 491-506). St. Louis, MO: C. V. Mosby.

DePaulo, B. M., Kenny, D. A., Hoover, C. W., Webb, W., & Oliver, P. V. (1987). Accuracy of person perception: Do people know what kinds of impressions they convey? *Journal of Personality and Social Psychology, 52*(2), 303-315.

Devereux, G. (1967). Professional defenses. In *From anxiety to method in the behavioral sciences* (pp. 83-96). The Hague, The Netherlands: Mouton.

Devore, W. (1985). Developing ethnic sensitivity for the counseling process: A social work perspective. In P. Pedersen (Ed.), *Handbook of crosscultural counseling and therapy* (pp. 93-98). Westport, CT: Greenwood.

Dodson, J. (1988). Conceptualizations of black families. In H. P. McAdoo (Ed.), *Black families* (pp. 77-90). Newbury Park, CA: Sage.

Dougherty, M. C. (1985). Anthropologists in nursing education programs. In C. E. Hill (Ed.), *Training manual in medical anthropology* (pp. 58-69). Washington, DC: American Anthropological Association.

Draguns, J. A. (1981). Counseling across cultures: Common themes and distinct approaches. In P. Pedersen, J. Draguns, W. Lonner, & J. Trimble (Eds.), *Counseling across cultures* (pp. 3-21). Honolulu: University Press of Hawaii.

Dressler, W. W. (1991). *Stress and adaptation in the context of culture: Depression in a southern black community.* Albany: The State University of New York Press.

Dyer, J., Vedlitz, A., & Worchel, S. (1989). Social distance among racial and ethnic groups in Texas: Some demographic correlates. *Social Science Quarterly, 70,* 607-616.

Eaton, E. (1982). *The shaman and the medicine wheel.* Wheaton, IL: The Theosophical Publishing House.

Farley, E. S. (1988). Cultural diversity in health care: The education of future practitioners. In W. A. Van Horne & T. V. Tonnesen (Eds.), *Ethnicity and health* (pp. 36-57). Milwaukee: The University of Wisconsin System Institute on Race and Ethnicity.

Fernandez, R. R., & Velez, W. (1985). Race, color, and language in the changing public schools. In L. Maldonado & J. Moore, (Eds.), *Urban ethnicity in the United States: New immigrants and old minorities* (pp. 123-143). Beverly Hills, CA: Sage.

Fine, M. (1982). When nonvictims derogate: Powerlessness in the helping professions. *Personality and Social Psychology Bulletin, 8*(4), 637-643.

Finn, C. E. (1990, June). Why can't colleges convey our diverse culture's unifying themes? *The Chronicle of Higher Education,* 15a.

Fiske, S. T. (1989, May 31). Court ruling against sex stereotyping in employment decisions will make it easier for professors to win discrimination lawsuits. *The Chronicle of Higher Education,* B-1, B-2.

Flaskerud, J. H. (1989). Transcultural concepts in mental health nursing. In J. S. Boyle & M. M. Andrews, (Eds.), *Transcultural concepts in nursing care* (pp. 243-269). Glenview, IL: Scott, Foresman.

Foster, B. L., & White, G. M. (1982). Ethnic identity and perceived distance between ethnic categories. *Human Organization, 41*(2), 121-130.

Foster, G. M., & Anderson, B. G. (1978). *Medical anthropology.* New York: John Wiley.

Foucault, M. (1980). *Power/knowledge, selected interviews and other writings 1972-1977.* Brighton, UK: Harvester House.

Frazier, R. J. (1987, August). Is the black middle class blowing it? . . . No. *Ebony,* pp. 89-90.

Freeman, J. (1984). *Women: A feminist perspective.* Palo Alto, CA: Mayfield.

Freidson, E. (1970). *Professional dominance: The social structure of medical care.* Hawthorne, NY: Aldine.

Gadow, S. A. (1985). Nurse and patient: The caring relationship. In A. H. Bishop & J. R. Scudder, (Eds.), *Caring, curing, coping* (pp. 31-43). Birmingham: University of Alabama Press.

Gadow, S. A. (1989). Clinical subjectivity: Advocacy with silent patients. *Nursing Clinics of North America, 24,* 535-541.

Gaines, A. D. (1982). Knowledge and practice: Anthropological ideas and psychiatric practice. In N. Chrisman & T. Maretzki (Eds.), *Clinically applied anthropology* (pp. 243-273). Dordrecht, The Netherlands: D. Reidel.

Galanti, G. A. (1991). *Caring for patients from different cultures: Case studies from American hospitals.* Philadelphia: University of Pennsylvania Press.

Gary, L. E. (Ed.). (1981). *Black men.* Beverly Hills, CA: Sage.

Gecas, V. (1982). The self-concept. *American Review of Sociology, 8,* 1-33.

Geller, J. D. (1988). Racial bias in the evaluation of patients for psychotherapy. In L. Comas-Diaz & E. E. H. Griffith, (Eds.), *Clinical guidelines in cross-cultural mental health* (pp. 112-134). New York: John Wiley.

Gergen, K. J., & Gergen, M. M. (1982). Explaining human conduct: Form and function. In P. F. Secord (Ed.), *Explaining human behavior* (pp. 127-154). Beverly Hills, CA: Sage.

Gibbs, J. T. (1984). Black adolescents and youth: An endangered species. *American Journal of Orthopsychiatry, 54,* 6-20.

Gite, L. (1986, November). Black men and suicide. *Essence,* pp. 130-134.

Goffman, E. (1956). *The presentation of self in everyday life.* New York: Doubleday.

Goffman, E. (1967). *Interaction ritual.* Garden City, NY: Anchor.

Goffman, E. (1969). *Strategic interaction.* Philadelphia: University of Pennsylvania Press.

Gorrie, M. (1989). Reaching clients through cross cultural education. *Journal of Gerontological Nursing, 15*(10), 29-31.

Greenleaf, N. P. (1980). Sex-segregated occupations: Relevance for nursing. *Advances in Nursing Science, 2*(3), 23-38.

Gudykunst, W. B. (1986). Ethnicity, types of relationship, and intraethnic and interethnic uncertainty reduction. In Y. Y. Kim, (Ed.), *Interethnic communication: Current research* (pp. 201-224). Newbury Park, CA: Sage.

Guthrie, B. (1988). The interrelatedness of the caring patterns in black children and caring process within black families. In M. Leininger (Ed.), *Caring: An essential human need* (pp. 103-107). Detroit: Wayne State University Press.

Hahn, R. A., & Gaines, A. D. (1985). *Physicians of modern medicine: Anthropological approaches to theory and practice.* Dordrecht, The Netherlands: D. Reidel.

Hamill, P. (1988, March). Breaking the silence: A letter to a black friend. *Esquire,* pp. 91-94, 96, 98, 100, 102.

Hammerschlag, C. A. (1988). *The dancing healers: A doctor's journey of healing with Native Americans.* New York: Harper & Row.

Hare, N. (1987, August). Is the black middle class blowing it? . . . Yes. *Ebony,* pp. 85-86.

Helman, C. G. (1990). *Culture, health and illness: An introduction for health professionals.* London: Wright.

Henry, W. A. (1990, April 9). Beyond the melting pot. *Time,* pp. 28-31.

Hewitt, J. P. (1984). *Self and society: A symbolic interactionist social psychology.* Boston: Allyn & Bacon.

Hill, R. B. (1987, August). The black middle class defined. *Ebony,* pp. 30, 32.

Hines, P. M., & Boyd-Franklin, N. (1982). Black families. In M. McGoldrick, J. Pearce, & J. Giordano (Eds.), *Ethnicity and family therapy* (pp. 84-107). New York: Guilford.

Hirschfield, L. A. (1984). Hermeneutics and some lessons from anthropology. *Contemporary Sociology, 15,* 34-37.

Hirschi, T. (1983, Spring). Families and crime. *The Wilson Quarterly,* 132-139.

Hofstede, G. (1986). Cultural differences in teaching and learning. *International Journal of Intercultural Relations, 10,* 301-320.

Horner, S. (1991). Intersubjective co-presence in a caring model. In *Caring and nursing explorations in the feminist perspectives* (pp. 107-115). New York: National League for Nursing. (Pub. no. 14-2369)

Howard, M. C. (1986). *Contemporary cultural anthropology*. Boston: Little, Brown.

Hughes, C. C. (1990). Ethnopsychiatry. In T. M. Johnson & C. F. Sargent (Eds.), *Medical anthropology: A handbook of theory and method* (pp. 132-148). New York: Greenwood Press.

Hyman, R., & Rosoff, B. (1984). Matching learning and teaching styles: The jug and what's in it. *Theory into Practice, 23*, 35-43.

Ivey, A. (1980). *Counseling and psychotherapy: Skills, theories and practice*. Englewood Cliffs, NJ: Prentice-Hall.

Jackson, J. S., McCullough, W. R., & Gurin, G. (1988). Family, socialization environment, and identity development in black Americans. In H. P. McAdoo (Ed.), *Black families* (pp. 242-256). Newbury Park, CA: Sage.

Jackson, R. K. (1979). The effects of the organizational setting on ethnic nurses and clients. In ANA Commission on Human Rights, *A strategy for change*, pp. 72-97.

Jacobsen, F. M. (1988). Ethnocultural assessment. In L. Comas-Diaz & E. E. H. Griffith (Eds.), *Clinical guidelines in cross-cultural mental health* (pp. 135-147). New York: John Wiley.

Jarmon, C. (1980). Racial beliefs among Blacks and Whites. *Journal of Black Studies, 11*, 235-247.

Jaynes, G. D., & Williams, R. M. (Eds.). (1989). *A common destiny: Blacks and American Society*. Washington, DC: National Academy Press.

Johnson, T. M., & Sargent, C. F. (Eds.). (1990). *Medical anthropology: A handbook of theory and method*. New York: Greenwood Press.

Jones, J. M. (1981). The concept of racism and its changing reality. In B. P. Bowser & R. G. Hunt (Eds.), *Impacts of racism on white Americans* (pp. 27-49). Beverly Hills, CA: Sage.

Katzman, E. M., & Roberts, J. I. (1988). Nurse-physician conflicts as barriers to the enactment of nursing roles. *Western Journal of Nursing Research, 10*(5), 576-590.

Kavanagh, K. H. (1988). The cost of caring. *Human Organization, 47*(3), 242-251.

Kavanagh, K. H. (1991a). Social and cultural influences: Values and beliefs. In J. L. Creasia & B. Parker (Eds.). *Conceptual foundations of professional nursing practice* (pp. 167-186, 187-210). St. Louis, MO: C. V. Mosby.

Kavanagh, K. H. (1991b). Invisibility and selective avoidance: Gender and ethnicity in psychiatry and psychiatric nursing staff interaction. *Culture, Medicine, and Psychiatry, 15*, 245-274.

Kavanagh, W. G. (1990). Personal communication. U. S. Army Environmental Hygiene Agency, Aberdeen Proving Ground, Maryland.

Kendell, R. E. (1975). *The role of diagnosis in psychiatry*. Oxford, UK: Blackwell.

Killian, L. M. (1981). Black power and white reactions: The revitalization of race-thinking in the United States. *Annals of the American Academy of Political and Social Science, 454*, 42-54.

Kim, Y. Y. (1988). On theorizing intercultural communication. In Y. Y. Kim & W. B. Gudykunst (Eds.), *Theories in intercultural communication* (pp. 11-21). Newbury Park, CA: Sage.

Kleinman, A. (1977). Rethinking the social and cultural context of psychopathology and psychiatric care. In T. Manschreck & A. Kleinman (Eds.), *Renewal in psychiatry: A critical rational perspective* (pp. 97-138). Washington, DC: Hemisphere.

Kleinman, A. (1978). Clinical relevance of anthropological and cross-cultural research: Concepts and strategies. *American Journal of Psychiatry, 135*(4), 427-431.

Kleinman, A. (1980). *Patients and healers in the context of culture: An exploration of the borderland between anthropology, medicine and psychiatry.* Berkeley: University of California Press.

Kolodny, A. (1991, February 6). Colleges must recognize students' cognitive styles and cultural backgrounds. *The Chronicle of Higher Education*, p. A44.

Korda, M. (1975). *Power! How to get it. How to use it.* New York: Random House.

Kourvetaris, G. A. (1978). The Greek American family. In C. H. Mindel & R. A. Habenstein (Eds.), *Ethnic families in America: Patterns and variations* (pp. 168-191). New York: Elsevier.

Kramer, J. M. (1988). Infant mortality and risk factors among American Indians compared to black and white rates: Implications for policy change. In W. A. Van Horne & T. V. Tonnesen (Eds.), *Ethnicity and health* (pp. 89-115). Milwaukee: University of Wisconsin System Institute on Race and Ethnicity.

Kuhn, M. H. (1964). Major trends in symbolic interaction theory in the past twenty-five years. *Sociological Quarterly, 5*, 61-84.

Kuhn, S., & Bluestone, B. (1987). Economic restructuring and female labor market: The impact of industrial change on women. In L. Beneria & C. R. Stimpson (Eds.), *Women, households, and the economy* (pp. 3-32). New Brunswick, NJ: Rutgers University.

Kumin, M. (1983, May 7). Carla: "It's very hard to say I'm poor." *The Nation*. Reprinted in W. Barnes (Ed.), *Social problems 85/86* (pp. 131-134). Guilford, CT: Dushkin.

Landy, D. (1977). The patient: Status and role. In D. Landy, (Ed.), *Culture, disease, and healing: Studies in medical anthropology* (pp. 385-388). New York: Macmillan.

Langer, E. J. (1983). *The psychology of control.* Beverly Hills, CA: Sage.

Lappin, J., & Scott, S. (1982). Intervention in a Vietnamese refugee family. In M. McGoldrick, J. Pearce, & J. Giordano (Eds.), *Ethnicity and family therapy* (pp. 483-491). New York: Guilford.

Larson, P. (1987). Comparison of cancer patients' and professional nurses' perceptions of important caring behaviors. *Heart Lung, 16*(2), 187-193.

Laughlin, W. S. (1963). Primitive theory of medicine: Empirical knowledge. In I. Galdston (Ed.), *Man's image in medicine and anthropology* (pp. 116-140). New York: International University Press.

Leavy, W. (1983, August). Is the black male an endangered species? *Ebony*, pp. 41, 42, 44, 46.

Lefley, H. P. (1984). Delivering mental health services across cultures.In P. Pedersen, N. Sartorius, & A. Marsella (Eds.), *Mental health services: The cross-cultural context* (pp. 135-171). Beverly Hills, CA: Sage.

Leininger, M. (1978). The significance of cultural concepts in nursing and excerpts from cultural differences among staff members and the impact on patient care. In M. Leininger (Ed.), *Transcultural nursing: Concepts, theories, and practices* (pp. 121-137). New York: John Wiley.

Leininger, M. (1981). Cross-cultural hypothetical functions of caring and nursing care. In M. M. Leininger (Ed.), *Caring: An essential human need; Proceedings of three national caring conferences* (pp. 95-102). Thorofare, NJ: Slack.

Leininger, M. (1984). Care: The essence of nursing and health. In M. M. Leininger (Ed.), *Care: The essence of nursing and health* (pp. 3-15). Thorofare, NJ: Slack.

Leininger, M. (1985a). The transcultural nurse specialist: Imperative in today's world. *Nursing & Health Care, 10*(5), 251-256.

Leininger, M. (1985b). *Qualitative research methods in nursing.* Orlando, FL: Grune & Stratton.

Leininger, M. (1985c). Transcultural caring: A different way to help people. In P. Pedersen (Ed.), *Handbook of cross-cultural counseling and therapy* (pp. 107-115). Westport, CT: Greenwood.

Leininger, M. (1988a). The phenomenon of caring: Importance, research questions and theoretical considerations. In *Caring: An essential human need* (pp. 3-15). Detroit: Wayne State University Press.

Leininger, M. M. (1988b). Leininger's theory of nursing: Cultural care diversity and universality. *Nursing Science Quarterly, 1*(4), 152-160.

Leininger, M. M. (1989). The transcultural nurse specialist: Imperative in today's world. *Nursing and Health Care, 10*(5), 251-256.

Leininger, M. M. (1991, April-May). Transcultural nursing: The study and practice field. *NSNA/Imprint,* pp. 55-66.

Levinson, D. (1989). *Family violence in cross-cultural perspective.* Newbury Park, CA: Sage.

Lieb, R. (1978). Power, powerlessness, and potential—Nurse's role within the health care delivery system. *Image, 10*(3), 75-83.

Lieban, R. W. (1974). Medical anthropology. In J. J. Honigmann (Ed.), *Handbook of social and cultural anthropology* (pp. 1031-1072). Chicago: Rand McNally.

Linton, R. (1936). *The study of man.* New York: Appleton-Century.

Liu, W. T., & Yu, E. S. H. (1985). Ethnicity, mental health and the urban delivery system. In L. Maldonado & J. Moore (Eds.), *Urban ethnicity in the United States: New immigrants and old minorities* (pp. 211-247). Beverly Hills, CA: Sage.

Lorion, R. P., & Parron, D. L. (1985). Countering the counter-transference: A strategy for treating the untreatable. In P. Pedersen (Ed.), *Handbook of cross-cultural counseling and therapy* (pp. 79-86). Westport, CT: Greenwood.

Lovell, M. C. (1981). Silent by perfect 'partners': Medicine's use and abuse of women. *Advances in Nursing Science, 33*(2), 25-40.

Lum, D. (1986). *Social work practice and people of color: A process-stage approach.* Belmont, CA: Brooks/Cole.

Manns, W. (1988). Supportive roles of significant others in black families. In H. P. McAdoo (Ed.), *Black families* (pp. 270-283). Newbury Park, CA: Sage.

Marshall, M. (1987, September). The alarming decline in the number of black college students. *Ebony,* pp. 44, 46, 48.

Martin, S. (1983). *Managing without managers: Alternative work arrangements in public organizations.* Beverly Hills, CA: Sage.

Masson, V. (1985, March-April). Nurses and doctors as healers. *Nursing Outlook,* pp. 70-73.

Maxwell, N. L. (1989). Demographic and economic determinants of United States income inequality. *Social Science Quarterly, 70*(2), 245-264.

McAdoo, H. P. (Ed.). (1988). *Black families.* Newbury Park, CA: Sage.

McElroy, A., & Townsend, P. K. (1989). *Medical anthropology in ecological perspective.* Boulder, CO: Westview.

McGoldrick, M. (1982). Ethnicity and family therapy: An overview. In M. McGoldrick, J. Pearce, & J. Giordano (Eds.), *Ethnicity and family therapy* (pp. 3-30). New York: Guilford.

McLanahan, S., & Garfinkel, I. (1989, January). Single mothers, the underclass, and social policy. *The Annals of the American Academy of Political and Social Science, 501,* 92-104.

Mecca, A. M., Smelser, N. J., & Vasconcellos, J. (Eds.). (1989). *The social importance of self esteem.* Berkeley: University of California Press.

Milio, N. (1971). *9226 Kercheval: The storefront that did not burn.* Ann Arbor, MI: Ann Arbor Paperbacks.

Milkman, R. (1987). Women workers and the labor movement in hard times: Comparing the 1930s with the 1980s. In L. Beneria & C. R. Stimpson (Eds.), *Women, households, and the economy* (pp. 111-131). New Brunswick, NJ: Rutgers University Press.

Milner, D. (1983). *Children and race.* Beverly Hills, CA: Sage.

Monro, D. H. (1973). Relativism in ethics. In P. P. Wiener (Ed.), *Dictionary of the history of ideas* (pp. 70-74). New York: Scribner.

Monrroy, L. S. A., & Orque, M. S. (1983). Issues and strategies for change in nursing education, practice, and research in ethnic nursing care. In M. S. Orque, B. Bloch, & L. A. Monrroy (Eds.), *Ethnic nursing care* (pp. 379-401). St Louis: C. V. Mosby.

Morse, J. M., Bottorff, J., Neander, W., & Solberg, S. (1991). Comparative analysis of conceptualizations and theories of caring. *Image, 23*(2), 119-126.

Morse, J. M., Solberg, S. M., Neander, J. W. L., Bottorff, J. L., & Johnson, J. L. (1990). Concepts of caring and caring as a concept. *Advances in Nursing Science, 13*(1), 1-14.

Navarro, V. (1979). *Imperialism, health and medicine.* Farmingdale, NY: Baywood.

Neubeck, K. J. (1986). *Social problems: A critical approach.* New York: Random House.

Nolde, T., & Smillie, C. (1987). Planning and evaluation of cross-cultural health education activities. *Journal of Advanced Nursing, 12,* 159-165.

Ogbu, J. U. (1988). Black education: A cultural-ecological perspective. In H. P. McAdoo (Ed.), *Black families* (pp. 169-184). Newbury Park, CA: Sage.

Parreno, H., Sr. (1983). Ethnic minority women and nurses in the health care setting. In M. Orque, B. Bloch, & L. Monrroy (Eds.), *Ethnic nursing care: A multicultural approach* (pp. 301-327). St. Louis: C. V. Mosby.

Patton, M. Q. (1980). *Qualitative evaluation methods.* Beverly Hills, CA: Sage.

Pearce, D. M. (1984). Farewell to alms: Women's fare under welfare. In J. Freeman (Ed.), *Women: A feminist perspective* (pp. 502-515). Palo Alto, CA: Mayfield.

Pedersen, P. (1979). Course materials, DISC (Developing Interculturally Skilled Counselors) Project. Honolulu: University of Hawaii.

Pedersen, P. (1981). The cultural inclusiveness of counseling. In P. Pedersen, J. Draguns, W. Lonner, & J. Trimble (Eds.), *Counseling across cultures* (pp. 22-58). Honolulu: University Press of Hawaii.

Pedersen, P. (1988). The three stages of multicultural development: Awareness, knowledge, and skill. In P. Pedersen (Ed.), *A handbook for developing multicultural awareness* (pp. 3-18). Alexandria, VA: American Association for Counseling and Development.

Pedersen, P. B., Draguns, J. G., Lonner, W. J., & Trimble, J. E. (Eds.). (1981). *Counseling across cultures*. Honolulu: University Press of Hawaii.

Peters, M. F. (1988). Parenting in black families with young children: A historical perspective. In H. P. McAdoo (Ed.), *Black families* (pp. 228-241). Newbury Park, CA: Sage.

Pfifferling, J. H. (1981). A cultural prescription for medicocentrism. In L. Eisenberg & A. Kleinman (Eds.), *The relevance of social science for medicine* (pp. 197-222). Dordrecht, The Netherlands: D. Reidel.

Phinney, J. S., & Rotheram, M. J. (Eds.). (1987). Introduction. *Children's ethnic socialization: Pluralism and development*. Newbury Park, CA: Sage.

Pinderhughes, E. (1982). Afro-American families and the victim system. In M. McGoldrick, J. Pearce, & J. Giordano (Eds.), *Ethnicity and family therapy* (pp. 108-122). New York: Guilford.

Poussaint, A. F. (1982, August). What every black woman should know about black men. *Ebony*, pp. 36-37, 39-40.

Poussaint, A. F. (1987, August). The pride of success: Remembering their roots burdens many blacks in mainstream with feelings of either guilt or denial. *Ebony*, pp. 76, 78, 80.

Quality Education for Minorities Project. (1990, March). Education that works: An action plan for the education of minorities. In Why we are behind: Ten myths about the education of minority Americans. *Black Issues in Higher Education*, pp. 16-17.

Rathus, S. A. (1987). *Psychology*. New York: Holt, Rinehart & Winston.

Ray, M. A. (1987a). Health care economics and human caring in nursing. *Family and Community Health*, *10*(1), 35-43.

Ray, M. A. (1987b). Technological caring: A new model in critical care. *Dimensions of Critical Care Nursing*, *6*(3), 166-173.

Ray, M. A. (1989). The theory of bureaucratic caring for nursing practice in the organizational culture. *Nursing Administration Quarterly*, *13*(2), 31-42.

Regan, A. M., & Sedlacek, W. E. (1989). Changes in social commitment of university freshmen over a decade by race and gender. *Journal of the Freshman Year Experience*, *1*(2), 7-19.

Richardson, E. H. (1981). Cultural and historical perspectives in counseling American Indians. In D. W. Sue (Ed.), *Counseling the culturally different: Theory and practice* (pp. 216-255). New York: John Wiley.

Ritzer, G., Kammeyer, K. C. W., & Yetman, N. R. (1982). *Sociology: Experiencing a changing society*. Boston: Allyn & Bacon.

Roberts, S. J. (1983). Oppressed group behavior: Implications for nursing. *Advances in Nursing Science*, *5*(4), 21-30.

Rodwin, V. G. (1988). Inequalities in private and public health systems: The United States, France, Canada. In W. A. Van Horne & T. V. Tonnesen (Eds.), *Ethnicity and health* (pp. 12-35). Milwaukee: The University of Wisconsin System Institute on Race and Ethnicity.

Rogers, R. C. (1989). Ethnic differences in infant mortality: Fact or artifact? *Social Science Quarterly*, *70*(3), 642-649.

Romanucci-Ross, L., Moerman, D. E., & Tancredi, L. R. (1983). *The anthropology of medicine: From culture to method.* New York: Praeger.

Rosenberg, M. (1965). *Society and the adolescent self-image.* Princeton, NJ: Princeton University Press.

Rosenberg, M. (1981). The self concept: Social product and social force. In M. Rosenberg & R. Turner (Eds.), *Social psychology: Sociological perspectives* (pp. 593-624). New York: Basic Books.

Rothenberg, P. (1990). The construction, deconstruction, and reconstruction of difference. *Hypatia, 5*(1), 42-57.

Sarbaugh, L. E. (1988). A taxonomic approach to intercultural communication. In Y. Y. Kim & W. B. Gudykunst (Eds.), *Theories in intercultural communication* (pp. 22-38). Newbury Park, CA: Sage.

Scheflen, A. E. (1972). Control by scapegoating. In *Body language and social order* (pp. 159-170). Englewood Cliffs, NJ: Prentice-Hall.

Scheper-Hughes, N. (1987). *Child survival: Anthropological perspectives on the treatment and maltreatment of children.* Dordrecht, The Netherlands: D. Reidel.

Schofield, W. (1964). *Psychotherapy: The purchase of friendship.* Englewood Cliffs, NJ: Prentice-Hall.

Schroeder, M. A. K. (1981). Symbolic interactionism: A conceptual framework useful for nurses working with obese persons. *Image, 13*(10), 78-81.

Scott, C. S. (1981). Health and healing practices among five ethnic groups in Miami, Florida. In G. Henderson & M. Primeaux (Eds.), *Transcultural health care* (pp. 102-114). Reading, MA: Addison-Wesley.

Sedlacek, W. E. (1983, December). Teaching minority students. In J. H. Cones, J. F. Noonan, & D. Janha (Eds.), *Teaching minority students: New directions for teaching and learning* (No. 16, pp. 39-50). San Francisco: Jossey-Bass.

Sedlacek, W. E. (1988). Institutional racism and how to handle it. *Health Pathways, 10*(9), 4-6.

Sedlacek, W. E., & Brooks, G. C. (1976). *Racism in American education: A model for change.* Chicago: Nelson-Hall.

Semmes, C. E. (1985). Minority status and the problem of legitimacy. *Journal of Black Studies, 15*(3), 259-275.

Sennett, R., & Cobb, J. (1973). *The hidden injuries of class.* New York: Vintage.

Shon, S. P., & Ja, D. Y. (1982). Asian families. In M. McGoldrick, J. Pearce, & J. Giordano (Eds.), *Ethnicity and family therapy* (pp. 208-228). New York: Guilford.

Shortridge, K. (1984). Poverty is a woman's problem. In J. Freeman (Ed.), *Women: A feminist perspective* (pp. 492-515). Palo Alto, CA: Mayfield.

Sigelman, L., & Welch, S. (1991). *Black Americans' views of racial inequality: The dream deferred.* New York: Cambridge University Press.

Singer, P. (1977). *Traditional healing: New science or new colonialism?* (Essays in critique of medical anthropology). Buffalo, NY: Conch.

Snow, L. F. (1983). Traditional health beliefs and practices among lower class black Americans. *The Western Journal of Medicine, 139*(6), 820-828.

Spector, R. E. (1991). *Cultural diversity in health and illness.* Norwalk, CT: Appleton & Lange.

Spradley, B. W. (1991). *Readings in community health nursing.* Philadelphia: J. B. Lippincott.

Spurlock, J. (1986). Development of self-concept in Afro-American children. *Hospital and Community Psychiatry, 37*(1), 66-70.

Stanford University. (1989, March). *Final report of the university committee on minority issues: Building a multiracial, multicultural university community.* Stanford, CA: Stanford University.

Staples, R. (1983, August). Black male sexuality: Has it changed? *Ebony,* pp. 104, 106, 108, 110.

Stark, E. (1984, May). The unspeakable family secret. *Psychology Today,* pp. 40-42, 44-46.

Stein, H. F. (1990). Psychoanalytic perspectives. In T. M. Johnson & C. F. Sargent (Eds.), *Medical anthropology: A handbook of theory and method* (pp. 73-92). New York: Greenwood Press.

Steinberg, S. (1989). *The ethnic myth: Race, ethnicity, and class in America.* Boston: Beacon.

Steinmetz, S. (1988). *Duty bound: Elder abuse and family care.* Newbury Park, CA: Sage.

Strauss, A. (1956). *The social psychology of George Herbert Mead.* Chicago: University of Chicago Press.

Strauss, C. (1984). Beyond 'formal' versus 'informal' education: Uses of psychological theory in anthropological research. *Ethos, 12*(3), 195-222.

Sue, D. W. (1981). *Counseling the culturally different: Theory and practice.* New York: John Wiley.

Sullivan, H. S. (1937). A note on the implications of psychiatry: The study of personal relations for investigations in the social sciences. *American Journal of Sociology, 42,* 846-861.

Sullivan, H. S. (1953). *The interpersonal theory of psychiatry.* New York: Norton.

Sundeen, S. J., Stuart, G. W., Rankin, E. D., & Cohen, S. A. (1985). *Nurse-client interaction: Implementing the nursing process.* St. Louis: C. V. Mosby.

Takaki, R. (1987). *From different shores: Perspectives on race and ethnicity in America.* New York: Oxford University Press.

Tannen, D. (1990). *You don't understand: Women and men in conversation.* New York: William Morrow.

Tavris, C., & Wade, C. (1984). *The longest war: Sex differences in perspective.* Orlando, FL: Harcourt Brace Jovanovich.

Tax, S. (1990). Can world views mix? *Human Organization, 49*(3), 280-286.

Taylor, E. (1989, February 27). Time is not on their side. *Time,* p. 74.

Terry, R. W. (1970). *For Whites only.* Detroit: Eerdmans.

Terry, R. W. (1981). The negative impact on white values. In B. P. Bowser & R. G. Hunt (Eds.), *Impacts of racism on white Americans* (pp. 119-151). Beverly Hills, CA: Sage.

Thio, A. (1986). *Sociology.* New York: Harper & Row.

Thomas, A., & Sillen, S. (1979). *Racism and psychiatry.* Secaucus, NJ: Citadel.

Thomas, R. R. (1990, March-April). From Affirmative Action to affirming diversity. *Harvard Business Review,* pp. 107-117.

Tifft, S. (1989, June). Help for at-risk kids. *Time,* p. 51.

Tollett, K. S. (1989). Universal education, Blacks, and democracy: The expansion and contraction of educational opportunities. In W. A. Van Horne & T. V. Tonnesen (Eds.), *Race: Twentieth-century dilemmas—Twenty-first century progno-*

ses (pp. 49-92). Milwaukee: The University of Wisconsin System Institute on Race and Ethnicity.

Truax, C. B., & Carkhuff, R. B. (1967). *Toward effective counseling and psychotherapy: Training and practice.* Hawthorne, NY: Aldine.

Turner, B. S. (1987). *Medical power and social knowledge.* London, UK: Sage.

U. S. Department of Human Services. (1985, September). *The report of the Secretary's task force on black and minority health.* Volumes 1-8.

van Dijk, T. A. (1987). *Communicating racism: Ethnic prejudice in thought and talk.* Newbury Park, CA: Sage.

Voydanoff, P., & Majka, L. C. (Eds.). (1988). *Families and economic distress: Coping strategies and social policy.* Newbury Park, CA: Sage.

Wacquant, L. J. D., & Wilson, W. J. (1989). The cost of racial and class exclusion in the inner city. *Annals of the American Academy of Political and Social Science, 501,* 8-25.

Watson, J. (1985). *Nursing: Human science and human care.* New York: Appleton-Century-Crofts.

Watson, J. (1988a). Some issues related to a science of caring for nursing practice. In M. Leininger (Ed.), *Caring: An essential human need. Proceedings of the three national caring conferences* (pp. 61-67). Detroit: Wayne State University Press.

Watson, J. (1988b). *Human science and human care: A theory of nursing.* New York: National League for Nursing.

Watson, J. (1990). Caring knowledge and informed moral passion. *Advances in Nursing Science, 13*(1), 15-24.

Weaver, J. L., & Garrett, S. D. (1983). Sexism and racism in the American health care industry: A comparative analysis. In E. Fee (Ed.), *The politics of sex in medicine* (pp. 79-104). Farmingdale, NY: Baywood.

Weidman, H. H. (1973). *Implications of the culture broker concept for the delivery of health care.* Paper presented at the annual meeting of the Southern Anthropological Society, Wrightsville Beach, NC.

Welts, E. P. (1982). Greek families. In M. McGoldrick, J. Pearce, & J. Giordano (Eds.), *Ethnicity and family therapy* (pp. 269-288). New York: Guilford.

Wendell, S. (1990). Oppression and victimization: Choice and responsibility. *Hypatia, 5*(3), 15-46.

Wertlieb, E. C. (1985). Minority group status of the disabled. *Human Relations, 38*(11), 1047-1063.

Whitten, N. E., & Szwed, J. F. (1970). *Afro-American anthropology.* New York: The Free Press.

Williams, J. (1988, March 6). Raising black kids in a white world. *Washington Post,* pp. C-1, C-4, C-5.

Wilson, W. J. (1984, Spring). The black underclass. *The Wilson Quarterly,* pp. 88-89.

Wilson, W. J. (1987). *The truly disadvantaged: The inner city, the underclass, and public policy.* Chicago: University of Chicago Press.

Winnick, A. J. (1988). The changing distribution of income and wealth in the United States, 1960-1985: An examination of the movement toward two societies, "separate and unequal." In P. Voydanoff & L. C. Majka (Eds.), *Families and economic distress: Coping strategies and social policy* (pp. 232-260). Newbury Park, CA: Sage.

Wirth, L. (1938). Urbanism as a way of life. *American Journal of Sociology, 64,* pp. 1-24.

Woldemikael, T. M. (1987). Assertion versus accommodation: A comparative approach to intergroup relations. *American Behavioral Scientist, 30*(4), 411-429.

Wright, B. A. (1983). *Physical disability: A psychosocial approach.* New York: Harper & Row.

Wrong, D. H. (1988). *Power: Its forms, bases, and uses.* Chicago: University of Chicago Press.

Zola, I. K. (1981). Structural constraints in the doctor-patient relationship: The case of non-compliance. In L. Eisenberg & A. Kleinman (Eds.), *The relevance of social science for medicine* (pp. 241-252). Dordrecht, The Netherlands: D. Reidel.

Index

About the Authors

Kathryn Hopkins Kavanagh (Ph.D., University of California, San Francisco and Berkeley; M.S. and M.A., University of Hawaii; B.S.N., Niagara University) is a former participant of the Developing Interculturally Skilled Counselors project at the University of Hawaii and previously taught cross-cultural counseling in Boston University's Masters of Educational Counseling program in Germany and the United Kingdom. With graduate degrees in psychiatric/mental health clinical nursing and medical anthropology, she is currently on the faculty at the University of Maryland at Baltimore School of Nursing, where she teaches transcultural nursing, medical anthropology, and qualitative research methods. Appointed by the governor as a member of the Maryland Ethnic Heritage Commission, she also chairs a grassroots, schoolwide group that is active in the promotion of diversity within the academic setting and nursing. Her primary scholarly interests focus on health care across cultures and diversity (particularly ethnicity) as it relates to health care. Current research projects emphasize peer counseling as a medium for HIV risk reduction among urban, drug-dependent women and a collection of oral histories of older African-American nurses in Maryland.

Patricia H. Kennedy (Ed.D., Catholic University, 1989) is Assistant Professor at the University of Maryland, School of Nursing where she received her undergraduate degree and master's in 1962 and 1963, respectively. Her Ed.D. is in Curriculum, Instruction, and Technology. The focus of her research has been ethics as it relates to teaching and learning and nurses' clinical decision making and on women who are abused by their partners. Within the last five years, in conjunction with colleagues, her activities have included systematic data collection about the minority experience and use of the results to influence school policy and to implement programs and workshops for faculty. Being a black woman and having been reared and educated entirely in the south, she has firsthand experience in coping with invisibility in integrated settings.